# WAR OF THE CHARIOTS

**CLIFFORD** allen **WILSON** 1923-

MASTER BOOKS
A DIVISION OF CLP
P.O. BOX 15666
SAN DIEGO, CALIFORNIA 92115

# THE WAR OF THE CHARIOTS

**MASTER BOOKS,** A Division of CLP
P. O. Box 15666
San Diego, California 92115

Library of Congress Catalog Card Number 78-55211
ISBN 0-89051-050-4

**Cataloging in Publication Data**

Wilson, Clifford A. 1923-
    War of the chariots.
    1. Interplanetary voyages. 2. Life on other planets.
    I. Daniken, Erich von, 1935-        Chariots of the gods? II. Title.


                            001.942                                    78-55211

Typeset in Australia; printed in the United States of America.

*Cover by Marvin Ross.*

*Printed by
El Camino Press
La Verne, California*

# The War of the Chariots

**is Clifford Wilson at his best!**

HERE ARE THE ANSWERS TO THOSE
QUESTIONS BEING ASKED AROUND
THE WORLD . . .

- How did the Dogon tribe know about the invisible star Sirius B?

- What about the Straw Man of the Kayapo Indians?

- Why did the Cosmonaut have bare feet?

- Did the Peruvian Indians attempt heart transplants?

- Where do U.F.O's come from?

- What about "Pyramidology" and "Pyramid Power"?

- Why blacks and whites?

35548

# Thanks for the Debate

CAMPUS ATTRACTIONS
NDSU Memorial Union
Fargo, North Dakota 58102

February 14, 1978

Dr. Clifford Wilson
Faculty of Education
Monash University
Clayton
Victoria, Australia

Dear Dr. Wilson:

Thank you very much for appearing on our campus this past weekend to debate Erich von Daniken. The program was very successful, with over 3,000 people present.

Our moderator, Dr. Jovan Brkic, has expressed his great appreciation for your presentation, your fluency, and your excellent command of English. Dr. John Hegaland, director of the School of Religion at North Dakota State University, said that your approach was very systematic and was effective in removing the presuppositions upon which von Daniken bases his thesis.

I congratulate you for a lucid and convincing message, one rooted in historical and archaeological fact, not mere conjecture.

Yours sincerely,

JARYL STRONG
Lectures Chairman
Campus Attractions

# THANKS...

To my wife Avis — who heard it all at North Dakota. She sold my books, but would not handle Erich von Daniken's at the autograph session!

. . . . . . . . . .

To my daughter Lynette Hallihan and my daughter-in-law Debra Wilson for the drawings, as follows:

# CONTENTS

**The Egyptian goddess Isis and the god Osiris, the god of the underworld. These are mentioned in Chapter 11.**

Osiris, the god of the night, was the counterpart of Ra the sun god. In Egyptian mythology Isis was a visible deity and Osiris the invisible Sirius B. There is a great deal of evidence to show that both Egyptians and Babylonians worshipped heavenly powers, and priests claimed to have knowledge from the gods, even as the Dogon tribe claims to have knowledge from the god Nommo.

(Osiris is also identified with Anubis, and so with Sirius A. Temple elaborates this very well at pages 62 ff.)

—Drawing by Lynette Hallihan

# Introduction . . .

## THE GREAT DEBATE IS PLANNED

I was in Australia, a long way from the action as they say. As a matter of fact, there's plenty of action in Australia too. I know. I come from there.

When the cable came from Jaryl Strong, Chairman of Campus Attractions at the North Dakota State University, I was a little surprised. "Campus Attractions" is a normal secular part of the University, and I had never met Jaryl Strong, but he knew of me as a writer. *Crash Go The Chariots* was now about five years old — surely there was not all that much public interest in the "Chariots" theme after so long? Then I remembered that Erich von Daniken had published several books, with total sales well over thirty millions.

I cabled my acceptance — yes, I was prepared to debate Erich von Daniken at the North Dakota State University. By now I had changed my contract with Monash University in Australia, and I was free to travel and lecture in the U.S. about half the time. So through my American contacts I arranged some other lectures, and eventually set out, with North Dakota my ultimate goal.

When I eventually arrived in Fargo, North Dakota, the snow was lying several feet deep. It seemed hardly the time or the place for a debate! Perhaps we were in for a really horrible flop! Indeed, I thought, maybe von Daniken would not be able to get into the place. Avis and I had come in via Minneapolis the day before the debate itself, and one of the TV interviews already had to be cancelled, because our earlier flight was itself cancelled because of the bad weather conditions. We sat around Minneapolis Airport for hours, hoping conditions would improve. They did, and we arrived in good time for the press, radio and television interviews in the afternoon.

Von Daniken got in all right, coming from another direction, and we met personally for the first time. I had actually debated him for about 25 minutes in Melbourne, Australia, some years ago, but that was a radio hook-up and we did not meet personally.

When we did meet in Fargo, I was somewhat surprised. He is rather short, seeming to bounce on his feet — he is the proverbial ball of energy, and at a personal level is quite a charming man. We got on well enough together, both that day and through to the end of the debate and his departure.

## Diametrically Opposed Views

Nevertheless we are diametrically opposed in basic beliefs, and that became even clearer as a result of that debate. It certainly will be clear throughout the pages of this book.

In a way I would like to include everything he said in the debate, but in giving me written permission (for which I paid) to use the material in various ways, such as a tape or film, he expressly stated that it was not for a book. I have the right to use my own material of course, and to quote sufficient of his material to explain what I am answering, and to summarize what was after all a public presentation. That I have done as the subject unfolds.

An edited version of the tape has been made, and is available through Word of Truth Productions, Box 288, Ballston Spa, N.Y. 12020, or by contacting the publishers of this book.

At last the time arrived, and it was gratifying to see the crowds streaming into the auditorium. The debate had been well advertized, with large posters seeming to hit us all over the city. To see such numbers of people on a bitterly cold winter's night, with snow piled up several feet, was an indication of very great and continuing interest. As I have already said, it surprised me, but of course I was glad to be involved. I believe in my answers to the way-out hypotheses of *Chariots Of The Gods?* and the rest of the von Danikenitis.

# Chapter 1:

## Von Daniken's Hour: Part 1 —
## HIS BASIC PREMISE

TO SOME WHO FOLLOW THIS ARGUMENT, THIS CHAP-
TER MIGHT SEEM UNINTERESTING. IT DEALS WITH VON
DANIKEN'S BASIC HYPOTHESIS RELATING TO CREATION BY
SPACE-GODS. HE SAYS SOME SURPRISING THINGS THAT
ARE CLEARLY THEOLOGICAL IN NATURE.

As von Daniken's hypothesis cannot be understood
without considering this matter, we do so in this chapter.
In the next chapter we proceed to other types of evidence
he presented at North Dakota.

The official figure was 3,200 attending the debate
at North Dakota State University. The cards handed in
showed that about 70% favored Erich von Daniken's
views before the debate began.

This was partly because von Daniken was known
world-wide. Wilson was not. His *Crash Go The Chariots*
had been a best-seller, but the New York publishers
(Lancer Books) had gone bankrupt at just the time of
*Crash Go The Chariots* being so successful. It was their
one best-seller, and the book was "frozen" for three years
as a result of the legal position.

The other side of the picture is that it surely is a
reflection on modern society that a large audience, pre-
dominantly made up of University students, would have
swallowed such large doses of von Danikenisms.

It is relevant to add that those same cards showed
that any type of change of viewpoint after the debate
were 50 to 21 in favor of Wilson, this being the official
figure given by the Chairman of Campus Attractions.
(A typical change was from "undecided" to either one
of the speakers.) Perhaps it is still true that though you
can fool some of the people all of the time, and all of
the people some of the time, you can't fool all of the
people all of the time!

Von Daniken and Wilson tossed a coin to see who

would speak first.  Wilson won, and elected to speak
AFTER von Daniken had given his initial address.

The Moderator for the evening was Professor Jovan
Brkic (pronounced as in Ber), Chairman of the University's Philosophy Department, and he introduced the
speakers and explained the format.  Von Daniken was
to speak for an hour, Wilson for an hour, von Daniken
to rebut for 15 minutes, Wilson for 15 minutes; von
Daniken again for 5 minutes, Wilson for 5 minutes; and
then 45 minutes of questions from the audience.  These
were to be put into two separate containers, one for each
speaker, and then the Moderator would select them
randomly, alternately from each container.  The person
addressed could speak for three minutes, and then the
other speaker could respond for three minutes if he so
chose.  There were to be brief intermissions throughout
the prescribed four hours.

Despite the late start, most of the format was
adhered to except for the 5-minute rebuttals.  These were
omitted because of time.

### The Question to be Debated

The question to be debated was: "Does the Historical
and Archaeological Evidence Support the Proposition
that Ancient Human Civilization was Influenced by
Astronauts from Outer Space?"

We shall see that he did NOT pursue this topic as
such, but merely pursued his own hypothesis.  Much
of what he said was really theological in nature.

The debate began.  Or at least, it nearly began, for
von Daniken thought his microphone was not working.
"Hullo, what's going on here?" he asked.  What he did
not realize was that there were two microphones —
one for the public address system and the other for the
official tape recording.  His microphone was all right,
but he had the two systems confused.

He quickly made a good point — that the question
of the debate "seems rather speculative."  That certainly
is true, for there is no proof whatever that earth has
been visited or influenced by astronauts from outer
space.

He went on to point out that in history there have
been other speculative things, and they have been proved
correct.  Many things that did not seem believable to

our grandparents have now been established as fact.
However, his argument is not totally acceptable when it
relates to "astronaut visits," nor does it follow a sequen-
tial pattern. Those previously speculative things associated with our grandparents' non-belief, to which von
Daniken referred, have now been shown to be fact.
On von Daniken's argument we should be able to say,
"Here is proof that was not available two generations
ago — proof about space visitors that was not available
in the days of our grandparents."

The facts belie such an argument. Von Daniken's
supposed evidences WERE available to our grandparents,
but passing time has DECREASED, not increased, the
possibility of outer space visits being the answer to
various so-called mysteries. We now know far more
about mysteries of the past than they did, and as knowledge increases it becomes even clearer that the answers
are very much earth-bound, with the "outer space visitors" hypothesis consistently rejected because it is
opposed by the evidence.

### Von Daniken's First Claim

Von Daniken's first claim was that in prehistoric and
early historic times earth was visited by unknown beings
from the universe.

This is immediately begging the question. He says
they were "unknown beings" — his words — and so he
throws his whole hypothesis into the melting pot. In
his various writings he has these "unknown beings"
coming from a number of space centers. Thus in
*Chariots Of The Gods?* he suggests Mars, or the Con-
stellation of the Pleiades, but in that same book he also
states that he does not yet know who these extra-terrestrial intelligences were, or from which planet they
came. He is making many jumps to conclusions based
on a starting "unknown" and including many other
unknowns as he proceeds.

So we come back to von Daniken's statement at
the debate. They are indeed "unknown beings." They
are unknown to von Daniken, to Wilson, and to all other
researchers. So far as the evidence allows such a forth-
right statement, they are unknown because they are
non-existent (unless we accept them as U.F.O. entities,
and von Daniken has made it clear he is not talking
about U.F.O.s).

Von Daniken's second point was that these unknown beings created human intelligence by a deliberate genetic mutation. He elaborated this theme at considerable length, coming back to it for a science fiction-type hypothesis later in his address.

He made the point that these extra-terrestrials "ennobled our forefathers in THEIR own image." He explains that it is not that THEY are like us, but that WE are like them.

## "After Their Own Image"

A number of the following points from von Daniken would not be acceptable to trained scientists. However, according to von Daniken . . .

Scientists say, "Yes, there is life out there." But why should these extra-terrestrials be in any way similar to us? The possibilities of life must be completely different, so why should such beings think similarly to us, or have similar technology? Why should they look similar to us? They are not similar to us, but we are similar to them — because WE are the products of their visit, and not the other way around.

Mythologies say that the gods created us after THEIR own image. "They created, by a deliberate mutation, our type of intelligence. We grow up in the same direction."

"It has been said, 'Why should extra-terrestrials visit exactly the earth?' I mean, in our galaxy we have billions and billions of solar systems — why exactly the earth? Well, I call this 'the exactly I syndrome'."

An illustration of the "exactly I" syndrome is where a person has cancer, and asks "Why should exactly I have this?" He does not know that others have the same sickness.

Von Daniken relates this to space beings. We say there are no others, but we simply do not know of societies in other solar systems, and so "we are not in a position to believe that only and exactly we have been visited." These visits to earth by alien beings from the universe were recorded and handed down in religions, mythologies and popular legends. This is the recurring theme of von Daniken's various books.

## Three Possible Reasons for the "Visits"

As we bring together the debate at North Dakota and *Gods From Outer Space* we find that he talks about time dilation, interstellar space travel, intermediate space stations, and space ships travelling just below the speed of light.

We are also asked why someone would come to earth and create our intelligence. What interest could there be in making stupid apes intelligent? We do not know a final answer, but there are several possibilities. According to von Daniken three of them are:

1. The aliens had an accident in space, and then they landed on our planet as the nearest possible landing place. As one result, they set out to make some of the "stupid apes" intelligent.

2. They needed manpower, and so they chose a planet similar to their own. They would not be able to get help from their own planet, for it was several light years away. Even if workers were available from the home base, they would not be familiar with our atmospheric and bacterial conditions. With the necessary genetic information available, it would be desirable to change the local beings into their own image by a deliberate mutation, and so produce "living working machines." "It is a speculative possibility."

3. The secrets of time and space. . . . There are extremely great differences of space between the solar systems of the universe. One possibility would be to construct a gigantic space station, with several generations living there — successive generations would reach the next space station. The only other possibility is, fantastic speeds.

**"If there is no Life . . . you Create it . . . it is Simple"**

"We have not the knowledge or the energy today. A team in a space ship have time that is different from the starting planet."

Von Daniken confidently tells us, "Theoretically, it would be possible for the rocket crew, maybe only 20 years pass, and on the starting planet 100,000 years."

(This concept of time virtually standing still is an Einstein concept that applies theoretically when about .9 of the speed of light (186,000 miles per second) is reached. To say the least von Daniken's hypothesis is highly controversial when applied to space travel at about 18,000 miles per hour, which is five miles per second — a long way from .9 of 186,000!)

Von Daniken further challenges us to speculate. We quote him extensively because we want it understood clearly that it IS what he said.

"Imagine society now. Because of scientific curiosity they want to visit Solar System No. 2. They want to find out, Are we alone? How do the others look like? Questions about God, and the beginning of the universe, and all this. So they send out a high speed space-ship. Now the scientists know very well that the answers will never come back, because when the rocket crew comes back from Solar System No. 2, there is nobody living on No. 1 — 100,000 years may be gone. So it seems to make no sense at all to make space travel with high speed — at least not for scientific knowledge. Except if they use the trick, if they said to the rocket crew, 'Well, you must not only visit Solar System No. 2, but during your own life span you have to visit all other possible solar systems, and on every solar system you look for forms of life."

"If there is no life, you create it. I mean, it is simple by the meaning of bacterias — just a little box would be enough to start evolution. If there is life, developed life, take the most advanced form of life, and change them by deliberate mutation after our own image — that means Society No. 1. It doesn't mean that they look exactly like we. Maybe they have three eyes, 7 fingers — I don't know. But after the genetic mutation they are intelligent. Before, they are not. The brain works similar to Society No. 1."

"If they do so in several solar systems they will finally win the game against time, and now it is possible to bring the answers back, though Solar System No. 1 to Solar System No. 2 may be 100,000 years away. . . . No. 2 to No. 3 may be a shorter distance . . . No. 3 and 4 — and again another distance. Simply create on several solar systems intelligence after their own image."

### In Space "a Whole Chain" is Needed

So suggested von Daniken at the North Dakota debate. "If you have one starting planet on the universe it may never work. You need a whole chain of it spread

out in time, so this could have been a very good reason
why they did it. And believe it or not, we will repeat
the same game. We have no alternative. We are intelligent — the only intelligent race on this planet . . .
Which by the way is proof enough."

"Proof enough" of what? Sometimes von Daniken's
meaning is not quite clear, but the basic hypothesis is
obvious enough. We do not have the authority to edit
his work, and so in this case the exact words have been
retained.

Add to all this von Daniken's public insistence (at
the debate) that he is not an atheist but is a firm believer
in a god, and we have an interesting situation. "I am
not an atheist at all," he declared. He made it clear,
however, that he did not accept the God of the Bible
Who (he wrongly claimed) is always associated with
demonstrations of power and noise, fire and thunder.

He stated that the apparition "never happens without smoke, fire, trembling, and loud noises. You can
look up in every passage in the Old Testament — whenever the mighty God descends, He crashes." He suggested that we do not need noise and other demonstrations of power like that in the 20th Century. The true
God is timeless, knowing yesterday, today and tomorrow.

He develops this further at pages 206 to 210 of
*According To The Evidence*. It is reasonable to ask,
What noise was associated with God's revelations to
Joseph who interpreted a Pharaoh's dream? Or with
Nathan's message to King David about David's sin with
Bathsheba? Or in relation to Daniel's understanding of
Nebuchadnezzar's vision? . . . Always noise? Von
Daniken is wrong as to his statements of facts, and his
interpretations are not only offensive to Christians: they
are distortions that are not objective, showing little grasp
of the balanced arguments of theology.

We have said enough as to his beliefs, and as we
analyze some of his statements it becomes clear that he
is arguing for a whole series of impossibilities, incredible
developments, and/or personal conjectures that are
totally incapable of proof. On the very figures von
Daniken himself gives relating to the amazing complexity
of a human cell, the possibility of chance human evolution is infinitesimally small. He acknowledges this.

Wilson agrees there are incredible odds against a cell

surviving, reproducing itself millions of millions of times — in a world that was totally mineral, with no soil or organic matter around it, no micro-organisms. The evidence is indeed so overwhelming that a God-figure is required. Creation, not chance evolution, is ultimately demanded. Von Daniken acknowledges this and clearly states, "I am not an atheist at all." However, as we have said, he does not accept the God of the Bible, but instead has a whole series of his own strange "creations."

## A List of Problems for von Daniken

Here is a list of some of the problems he encounters along the way:—

1. As he himself acknowledges in *According to the Evidence*, chance evolution is so improbable statistically, as to be virtually impossible. For it to have happened a number of times (as he conjectures), brings the statistical possibilities to the point of absurdity.

2. Von Daniken is therefore brought face to face with the need for an act or acts of creation. He uses the term "creation" in a much more limited way than in the Bible.

3. On each of his propounded "space stations" he already had ape-like beings. Obviously these did not have the "intelligence" (his word) to make it possible for them to move out from their habitation to another "space station." Thus we are to believe in a whole series of evolutionary developments having already taken place to a high standard (apes), BEFORE his separate acts of "creation" by space gods.

4. As the evolution of even one cell is virtually impossible, even according to his own arguments, the evolution of one ape on just one planet is vastly more incredible. However, he needs a chain of such creatures, existing separately, on a whole series of space stations.

5. Von Daniken's "creations" would involve a genuine God-figure, for such activity is totally beyond human or humanoid potential. Von Daniken is simply pushing the answer back one or more steps, and he comes up with a solution far less satisfying than that of the Bible.

6. Von Daniken's own quote of Nobel Prize winner Professor Max Perutz in *Gods From Outer Space* is relevant. Professor Perutz wrote (as quoted by von Daniken), "How could we erase a specific gene from one particular chromosome, or add one to it, or repair a single pair of nucleotides? It hardly seems practicable to me."

Von Daniken rejects that latter part of the quote: he quotes another authority who believes that "the difficulties can be overcome one day." He rejects that part of the statement by Professor Perutz that opposes his hypothesis, and in a way that is fair enough. Authorities will often differ on specific points, and if one searches long enough he will find another authority with a different view.

7.   He is far from convincing in his pseudo-biological argumentation.

He has insufficient data and makes his own use of scientific terminology as he comes to his way-out conclusions.

8.   Von Daniken is forced to renounce evolution and to accept a creationist position, but he throws up a wildly-conjectural hypothesis that both rejects and also accepts evolution at the one time. Evolution through cells to apes is impossible, yet space gods used those non-existent apes to create intelligent beings "in their own image."

9.   Von Daniken's "gods" are clearly very limited as gods go. They cannot communicate across vast distances; they need "manpower" to help in their projects; their machines are subject to breakdown; they are searching for the secrets of life; they are even searching for knowledge of God!

10.   The space beings did not create the original apes, and on von Daniken's arguments as to the impossibility of their evolution, logically we are forced back to a Creator Who created the animals, as well as having created man in His Own image.

11.   The God of the Bible has all the attributes to be expected of an Almighty Creator. He is omnipotent, all-powerful; He is omnipresent, everywhere present; He is omniscient, having all knowledge. By comparison, von Daniken's "gods" are indeed small in stature, with very limited abilities.

12.   The God of the Bible does not need a series of space stations as He investigates time and space. He is eternal, the Creator Who cannot be contained by space, and not merely the investigator of time and space!

13.   The fact is, von Daniken recognizes the need for a Creator-God, and has tried to create such a God in HIS image (the image of any fallen man). His concept of God is very much inferior to that given in the Old Testament.

14. Von Daniken's conjecture that the space-gods' visits have been recorded in mythologies, religious beliefs, and popular legends is unnecessary. A comparison of relevant "legends" with the Bible records consistently shows that those non-Biblical records and legends are corruptions, often containing grotesque absurdities. If we are prepared to be objective, the Bible records are acceptable to intelligent, thinking men, provided we accept the concept of God. That cannot be said of mythologies or sagas such as the Babylonian *Enuma Elish*, or the *Epic of Gilgamesh*, or the Egyptian creation myths.

## Eve Created in a Retort!

15. Von Daniken's conjectures about the creation of Adam and then the formation of Eve "in a retort" are so way-out that one wonders if the man is serious. Perhaps he is not. In the earlier radio encounter (with Wilson) he acknowledged that he put some things out "to be provocative."

Surely he is not serious when he relates the Genesis creation records to cave drawings about the mother goddess? Or the use of Adam's rib "as a cell culture" (of Eve), wherein the gods "brought the sperm to development in it?" So he goes on — then he tells us, "Nevertheless, the new men later mated with animals again . . ." (*Gods From Outer Space*, page 28.) Elsewhere he states in a direct contradiction to this, "What I should like to deny is that one species has been able to cross with another at any time in the course of evolution!" (*According To The Evidence*, page 237.)

This author (Wilson) does not always know when von Daniken is serious!

# Chapter 2:

# Von Daniken's Hour: Part 2 —
# SUPPORTING DATA AT
# NORTH DAKOTA

(We do not keep saying "Mr. von Daniken stated," but these are HIS opinions, not Wilson's.)

Von Daniken did not only talk about creation and evolution, though they were certainly prominent. Some of the topics he discussed were those already dealt with in his books.

## The Nazca Lines

He elaborated his views concerning the Nazca lines in Peru. The impression of an airfield was true, from a low altitude as well as from a high altitude, as though one was just about to land on a real runway. Earlier arguments such as the lines being old Inca roads, or a religion of trigonometry, or a huge astronomical calendar (as put forward by the German scientist Maria Reiche), must be put aside.

An American, Jim Woodman, had constructed a hot-air balloon, and he had finally succeeded in raising himself above the level of the plain, for a few seconds.

(It was not "for a few seconds": it was reported as rising 600 feet.)

Critics said that here was the answer — at last Erich von Daniken had been proved wrong, but in fact this balloon experiment could not even scratch his hypothesis. He had never claimed that the Incas had no hot-air balloons. Since when do hot-air balloons need runways?

(Wilson would like to know if vehicles from outer space would "need runways.")

## The Palenque "Astronaut"

The stone figure at Palenque in Mexico had a "masked" figure that looked like a racing motor cyclist. It was discovered in 1952. One authority had suggested that von Daniken should rotate the picture, lengthwise

instead of crosswise, but then it would have the vehicle
rising directly into the clouds. Such a rotation would
prove Mr. von Daniken right, he claimed. The picture
also depicts Venus, the moon symbol, the tree of life,
and a flame. In 1966 Dr. Wernher von Braun had commented that it looked like a man at the controls of his
space ship.

Earlier authorities had claimed that the picture depicted an Indian at a sacrificial altar, but now archaeologists say he is the ruler of Palenque. He is obviously
fairly well dressed, with a suit ending in cuffs at his
wrist, with his hands in a very precise position. It looks
as if his upper hand is winding up something. "Is it
really such a crime to interpret this magnificent drawing
technically? Well, a NASA engineer has done it, and
this is the result . . . I do not say that is the way it was.
No, I simply mean as long as we don't know for sure
what is true, we should be fair enough to give both
versions a possibility."

Mr. von Daniken had studied the archaeological
interpretation of this relief. He had also studied the
report of the man who discovered the stone. However,
taking into consideration the position of the hands only,
and remembering our intellectual freedom, we ask why
an Indian High Priest should sit at a sacrificial altar in
such a stupid position?

(Wilson points out the ruler's name, Pacal, is recorded right there, and the sarcophagus is dated to the
7th Century A.D. This is NOT an astronaut blasting off.)

Von Daniken admits "We do not know," but in
*Chariots Of The Gods?* he says, "today any child would
identify his vehicle as a rocket" (page 100). In the same
context he suggests it is the god Kukumatz. As stated
above, the inscriptions show it is the ruler Pacal.

### "I Saw Visions of God" Omitted

Mr. von Daniken read sections of Ezekiel Chapter 1,
dealing with Ezekiel's description of what Mr. von Daniken claimed was a space ship. The words, "I saw visions
of God" were omitted from the reading by Mr. von Daniken.

Ezekiel was not sure what he was talking about,
but described something AS the color of amber — he
did not say what the object was, but what it looked like.

Josef Blumrich was for 15 years one of the heads of NASA and had been involved during his life with airplanes, rockets and the space shuttle. He has tried to explain the alleged visions of the prophet Ezekiel. He concluded that a nuclear reactor was housed in the center, with a cooler for the reactor in the lower portion. These were necessary for the working of the four helicopter-type vehicles. The cooler would glow for hours after the space ship had stopped.

This is what the prophet Ezekiel states, "And out of the midst thereof — as the color of amber." When he referred to the four living creatures he was talking about the helicopters. He puts it more clearly later when he says he heard a rushing noise behind him: he heard the noise of the wings, and said that the rattle of the wheels sounded like the thundering of a waterfall.

### "Ezekiel is not having Visions"

"Ezekiel is not crazy. He is not having visions either. Being a brilliant observer, he is describing by words of his time what he is seeing and hearing." Ezekiel also described the space vehicle as "the splendidness of God," but on the contrary the commander is not designated as God. "He describes the commander, that he looks like the son of a man in his linen clothes. I would say he had a kind of space suit on. This space ship is supposed to be fired by the mother space craft outside of the atmosphere." Ezekiel is describing something he actually saw, and he got excited about it. It was a wheel that could go forward and backward, but not right and left, at the same time, without the execution of a steering movement. He says it was as if one wheel were in the middle of another wheel.

"In the universe, as well as in the upper atmospheric layers, helicopters and the rotary blades are clicked on," he told us. He described how the helicopters were let down at about 2,000 or 3,000 feet, the commander is then able to choose his landing site, and Ezekiel describes what he saw taking place.

He describes the helicopter's wheel for the first time, as an object that is known to him, and he got excited about it.

At NASA they had worked out what the wheel was, and had constructed one. "It is divided into different segments from the wheel's axis. Each segment ends in its own little axle. Each axle is able to spin in both directions, around to the left, or around to the right. It is easy to understand."

Mr. von Daniken countered the argument that this was his own interpretation by his conclusion (not further elaborated) that there is a lot of evidence for his conclusion.

(What a pity von Daniken ended his Bible reading in the middle of a sentence and omitted the words, "And I saw visions of God" — Ezekiel 1: 13. A vision is a spiritual and/or mental experience. Apparently others with Ezekiel did not share his implanted experience.)

(Also, von Daniken specifically stated in the debate, "He's not having visions." But Ezekiel says he was. I'll believe Ezekiel on this one!)

### The Straw Figure and the Kayapo Indians

In 1952 the Kayapo Indian tribe in Brazil were located. They have ritual straw garments that are supposed to symbolize visitors from space. One day a being came to their village, and because foreigners had to be accepted, he was welcomed. He learned the language of the inhabitants, and the tribes learned that his name meant "I am coming from the universe." He taught them tricks about hunting, gave them knowledge of agriculture, and built their first school. The tribe believes that one day there was a noise, and then some of the young warriors who had discreetly followed him saw him disappear into the clouds. In his memory the Indians wear straw garments in a ritual ceremony each year.

"May I use your imagination once more please," Mr. von Daniken asked. He suggested that if we thought someone had died out 200 years ago, and then we found these straw garments in their villages, how would we interpret them? But we are still here, alive, and they are able to tell us their story, in simple songs that have been unchanged in generations. This is not just an interpretation, but is a living mythology that continues today. These figures look similar to astronauts.

### The First Japanese Emperor

Mr. von Daniken went on to early Japanese culture, showing a figure he dated to about 600 B.C., known as a "dogu." They were in stone or clay, and are connected with mythology. The first Japanese Emperor ruled about this time. His name was Jimmu Tenno, and he was said to be a son of the gods, and was given the Japanese kingdom by the gods.

We have no problem in following von Daniken's argument at this point, for it is further elaborated in *According To The Evidence* (page 128). He tells us that the Japanese dogu figurines first emerged about 600 B.C., "And this was just the time when the gods of heaven gave Jimmu Tenno, the first emperor of Japan, his empire."

One Chinese tradition from mythology has a monkey being left behind on a voyage to the main island of Japan, and the Japanese people being its descendants. Now the gods of heaven are involved, even as they were with the early Sumerians. Such a statement would be taken as a figure of speech by many writers, but not by Erich von Daniken. By the same approach we should believe that the Egyptian Pharaohs were each separately descended from Ra the sun god.

The 600 B.C. date is no problem for von Daniken. It is approximately the same date as for Ezekiel, and so is at the time of von Daniken's third visit from spacemen "in Biblical times." The fact that this is about 800 years after Moses (who also supposedly talked to the space gods at the time of that same visit) is of no importance. Only true scholars would worry about THAT sort of problem!

### God Figures in Many Museums

Mr. von Daniken referred to god-like figures found in many museums. The Hopi Indians refer to the Kachinas as high spiritual beings from space who helped them in many practical ways, such as the building of statues in Mexico, with eyes like robots. The objects in their hands are held by two fingers and are supposed by archaeologists to be symbolic keys. They are god-like pieces that stare at us from the show-pieces of many museums. Such pieces are found in Lima, Peru and in the dry sands of the desert. We are always told that these are only toys or sports figures, or mythological characters. Mr. von Daniken agrees they are mythological characters — but what kind of mythology?

In the Middle Ages Christians built temples and produced art pieces, and they knew the God they were honoring. The people who made the gods in museums also knew which god they were honoring. This would be the case with such figures and cave paintings around the world, showing beings with helmets and haloes. Some are in northern Italy, made by stone age men, and there are others as far away as near Alice Springs in the center of Australia. They all show gods with helmets and space suits, and again neither had contacts with paintings depicting similar things in places such as Buckeye (in Arizona), and in Russia, and in the Sahara Desert, where there is a whole gallery of such drawings. All of these have helmets and space suits. Is all that nothing?

Our stone-age forefathers were naturalists, and we understand many of the paintings around the world. A naturalist is one who paints what he sees. The question is — naturalists, yes, but what was the model for this wall life? The hat is fixed with the body, so it could be a naturalist, but after what body?

(Recently this author (Wilson) watched as von Daniken showed a number of these "god-like figures" on TV. At the end the host commented, "Only one of them looked at all like a space-man" — it had something like a rectangular mask across its face, covering the eyes and nose. Many a First Grade child could draw better likenesses of "space-men."

In any case, that particular figure looks just as much like a masked bank robber as an astronaut.) (It is pictured at page 129 of *According To The Evidence*.)

### Where the Gods went to Heaven

In the midst of a rather symmetrical mountain near Santa Cruz in Bolivia there are two lines and nobody knows how to interpret them. The Indians there ascertained that the gods went to heaven on those lines. "What shall I say?" von Daniken asked, "A mount with a launching pad?" One archaeologist had suggested they are draining channels for cultural beer. (Mr. von Daniken does not say WHICH archaeologist!) Mr. von Daniken does not know, he told us, the meaning of the circles in his picture.

## The Dogons and the Sirius Mystery

Mr. von Daniken elaborated the mystery outlined by American linguist Robert Temple in his recent book *The Sirius Mystery*. Dr. Marcel Griaule, a French anthropologist, and ethnologist Dr. Germaine Dieterlen, published their article *A Sudanese Sirius System*. The two scholars had lived for several years among the Dogon tribe who live in the African Republic of Mali.

The Dogon tribe celebrate the Sigui Feast every 50 years. They worship an invisible star in the Sirius system. They do not mean the bright star Sirius itself, which has been known for thousands of years. They insist that they worship an invisible companion of Sirius. How can they worship an object that is invisible? They claim that the invisible companion is extremely small but is the heaviest body in the Sirius system. This star is called Po Tolo, "Po" referring to the smallest West African cereal grain in that area, and so is an appropriate name for this small companion.

The Dogons have an amazing knowledge of the invisible star. They describe its orbit, and say it is made of a very heavy metal.

In the middle of the 19th century the astronomer Bessel discovered that the movements of Sirius A were erratic. He concluded that an accompanying invisible star was affecting it. In 1862 (in *According To The Evidence*) the American astronomer Clarke proved Bessel correct, with Sirius B exactly where it had been predicted. It was not invisible, but had been outshone by its bright companion, Sirius A. Sirius B is a "white dwarf," very small, but of very high density, and it influences the motion of the much larger Sirius A. The two stars orbit each other every 50 earth years.

## Knowledge of a 50-year Cycle

The Dogon tribe have long had accurate knowledge of Sirius B, knowledge we have gained only in recent times. They knew of the 50-year cycle; they knew Sirius B was extremely small; they say Po Tolo (Sirius B) is made of a very heavy metal.

The Dogons say they got their precise knowledge from the creator Nommo. He visited the Dogons unknown generations ago, and gave them much knowledge in many fields, some of it still beyond our potential to verify.  For instance, they talk of other planets in the Sirius system.  One is called the Planet of Women, another, Planet of Shoemaker.

(One problem is that even Sirius A itself is not a "planet" — Wilson.)

The Sirius B evidence, according to Mr. von Daniken, is conclusive proof of visitors from outer space in the remote past.  Nobody could have known the details "understood" by the Dogon tribe.

## That Stone Library in Pictures

South of Lima in Peru there is an old city called Ica.  A very interesting museum is there, built up by Professor J. Cabrera, with 25,000 engraved stones, of various sizes.  It is called The Stone Library in Picture Form.  The stones were collected by the Indians in the region, mainly in the dry river bed.

## A Heart Transplant?

Mr. von Daniken went on to speculate that if 5,000 years ahead earth beings saw lights "up there," they would go out and investigate.  Those who created our intelligence know that sooner or later we will do it. As a child contacts its parents, so we will contact our space-creators.

Mr. von Daniken then commented that earlier he had not been able to show pictures from the "Stone Library."  He now went back to them.  Some of the pictures were of star maps, and others (which he now presented) seemed to show a man on a bed or an operating table.  Two other men are nearby, and they appear to be opening the first man's chest and taking something out.

"Could we anatomically present a heart any better today? he asked.  "Was it a sacrifice?  Was the heart treated from the body?  No.  It was a heart transplantation.  On the back side of the same stone there is another operating table with another patient.  Other surgeons are opening his chest, taking out his heart.  No. 2 has been brought to patient No. 1.  A new heart was inserted, the patient is obviously attached by a number of infusions to some sort of technical equipment.  The surgeons are closing chest and belly with needle and thread.  When I saw these stones with these pictures for the first time I suddenly felt Professor Barnard was not the first."

(We discuss this in Questions and Answers section. The pictures are QUITE CLEARLY fakes, and we present some evidence. In any case human hearts were offered in sacrifices.)

## Indians Worshipping a Ship in the Sky

Mr. von Daniken then showed a slide of a man riding a bird while he holds a saddle in his hand. It was a bigger bird than we know of in the past, but we should not forget that the place where these stones have been found is only six kilometers away from the picture of the huge bird.

"Airstrips — flame — birds — to end all this, a gigantic stone 1 meter .61 (it is 1.41 in *According To The Evidence* — Wilson) in height, all covered with engravings." There are stars, a comet, and Indians worshipping something in the sky. There are two other Indians who have a kind of tree between them, and they also are watching the sky. You will see "that the Indians watched the sky with telescopes . . . Between the stars up there, there is a ship." (This is also stated at page 332 of *According To The Evidence*.)

The Indians in this area know ships, for they live very close to the Pacific coast. "If they put a ship in between the stars, what would they mean with it? A ship is something of transportation — it is a medium of transportation, and if at the same time they are worshipping the ship, praying on their knees, what do they mean? I think the ship of the gods in the stars."

Mr. von Daniken said his hour had passed. We should remember:

(1) The Kayapo Indians with the straw garments "who tell us why they do it;" and

(2) The knowledge of the primitive Dogon tribe about Sirius B and its exact orbit.

"I think such indications would by far be convincing enough for a court of this planet for a verdict: the gods were astronauts."

# Chapter 3:

## WILSON'S CHALLENGE TO VON DANIKEN: PART 1 — ARCHAEOLOGY SHOWS MAN'S INTELLIGENCE

It would not be desirable to publish every word spoken by Clifford Wilson. Some of the argumentation is developed in greater detail in other parts of this book, and in any case both von Daniken and Wilson presented their material with accompanying colored slides, and obviously much that was said does not make particularly good sense without the slides being available. Thus we shall give an edited version of Wilson's address, with special reference to those parts that are most relevant.

### The Indian Pillar and an Ancient Map

Wilson commenced his hour's address by referring to the Indian pillar outside Delhi, and showed a picture of it. Von Daniken discusses it in *Chariots Of The Gods?* Wilson explained that the nearly pure iron found in that pillar was similar to the so-called bog iron found in New Jersey. He showed slides of various weapons of war made by people in ancient times, weapons that were surprisingly modern, and utilizing techniques that at times have only recently been known, such as the hardening process of bronze. No astronaut power was used.

He discussed the Piri Re'is map, and stated that he had a problem as to von Daniken's real belief. In the interview reported in *Playboy* magazine von Daniken is supposed to have changed his mind about the Piri Re'is map, as also about the Indian pillar. He had acknowledged that in both cases the "visitors from space hypothesis" did not apply after all. Wilson acknowledged that journal reports are not always reliable, and it was hard to know what Erich von Daniken really believed at this point, for von Daniken had again referred to the Piri Re'is map in his second book (apparently accepting it as evidence of an outer space visit after all).

*(In the rebuttal period later, von Daniken did not elaborate to show which of the two points of view he now held.)*

Wilson pointed out that the Piri Re'is map was not as fantastically accurate as von Daniken claimed. It had the River Amazon shown twice. South America was joined to Antarctica, and the map certainly was not the same as a satellite picture taken over Cairo.

Similarly, the great stones found at Baal-Bek, to which von Daniken referred in *Chariots Of The Gods?*, were remarkable, but they were man-made. Evidences of old-fashioned tooling as used by humans had been found, and faults in the famous huge stone left lying near a modern roadway had also been found. (That was why it was abandoned.)

## Do Archaeologists "Cement Down their Views"?

Wilson elaborated the ways in which archaeologists date their history, and showed something of pottery evidences such as the lamp, with distinctive patterns according to time periods of a particular culture. Von Daniken had written at great length about archaeologists cementing down their views and not being prepared to change their point of view. Wilson showed that even a man such as William Foxwell Albright, the very great "dean of Biblical archaeology," had dramatically changed his mind from time to time as the evidence so demanded, and had clearly stated where he had been wrong.

Some of the important finds of archaeology were touched on briefly, including the Rosetta Stone, famous for the ultimate deciphering of hieroglyphics; and the Behistun Stone in Ancient Persia, one of the milestones for the understanding of cuneiform. It was inscribed on a mountain-side above a trade-route, without astronaut help!

Colored slides were presented, illustrating that ancient people kept good records, such as in the Assyrian King List which named 107 early Assyrian Kings. Some of these kings had great palaces, such as those of Sargon and Sennacherib. Ashur-bani-pal had left behind a great library, with tablets collected widely from the ancient world.

The archaeological evidence for settled civilizations did not go back hundreds of thousands of years. Even according to Carbon 14 dating, which is not reliable beyond one half-life of about 5,700 years (if for that!), it goes back to only about 9,000 years ago. The Neolithic Tower at Ancient Jericho is a good demonstration that so-called "early man" built remarkable structures that could last through thousands of years. The fact is, the archaeological evidence shows that as soon as man is settled in his civilizations he has a tremendous capacity to build such structures, and had no need for astronaut help.

## Remarkable Evidences of Advanced Culture from Ur

Wilson stated, "Sometimes as we go through the history of ancient people we are staggered at what they were able to produce. For instance, the city of Ur, which was the center for the Biblical Abraham, was excavated by Sir Leonard Woolley. At a level 500 years before Abraham's time, amazing things were found. Some of the children went to school, cube root was known and utilized, and even Pythagoras' Theorem was known. The modern version of that theorem says that in a right-angled triangle the square on the hypotenuse is equal to the sum of the squares on the other two sides. These ancient people did not actually state that in our words, but they did show a right-angled triangle in a square that was bisected by the hypotenuse, and they gave a number of figures which made it clear that they thoroughly understood the principle.

"This was 500 years before the times of Abraham, and that means it was about 2,000 years before the Greek Pythagoras. The point we are making is, as soon as men are in their settled civilizations we find that they are intelligent. They have all sorts of technological know-how, and there is no need to look beyond the fact of intelligence to explain their accomplishments.

"Sir Leonard Woolley excavated the Royal death pits at Ur, and in them he found beautiful golden vessels. Those golden vessels were necessarily imported, for the people of Ur lived on land next to the Persian Gulf. There was 40 feet of clay beneath their feet, washed down with the silt from the two rivers: the Euphrates and the Tigris swept down and formed the great area of plain known in the Bible as the Plain of Shinar, and in archaeology as Sumer.

"These people did not get their gold from visitors from outer space, but they traded across the sea, and in the ancient city of Ur records were found about the

trading that they actually undertook. Their great
ziggurat (temple tower) was not only a place of worship,
but it was also a trading center, where spinning and
weaving and many other activities were constantly being
undertaken.

"They had magnificent musical instruments such
as the harp, dating hundreds of years before scholars
had thought such instruments had been known."

Wilson made the point that these were highly intelligent people just as soon as we are able to investigate
them: "Here are these people, whom we surely would
have thought were primitive: way back in early times
we have these villagers able to do remarkable things
with their clay (which was all they had in their natural
settings), such as the building of two-storeyed houses.
For other purposes they imported gold, and silver, and
so much more."

## "These Really are Gold!"

Wilson showed a whole series of golden implements,
and had a sly dig at von Daniken as he commented, "It
rather reminds me of some of the things that we have
in *Gold Of The Gods*, but these really ARE gold!"

(This was a reference to von Daniken's book *Gold
Of The Gods*, which has been seriously criticized because
the explorer and guide Juan Moricz was supposed to
have taken von Daniken into the tunnels. Moricz claimed
that they had never actually been inside the tunnels and
that there certainly was no golden zoo ever found in the
way described by von Daniken. In the *Encounter* magazine referred to earlier in this book, von Daniken
acknowledged that he had not been in the area claimed
by him, but argued that certain details could not be given
for the sake of keeping information secret, and that in
any case certain journalistic freedom was permissible.
That is very challengeable when one is putting out serious
material, or at least material that purports to be serious,
and is the supposed basis for (what he claimed was) a
revelation dealing with the actual writings about creation.
Moricz accused von Daniken of lies and "fudging" of
photographs.)

Wilson further used the culture at Ur to illustrate
the way ancient men and women were basically the same
as their modern counterparts. One example was the

golden jewellery dating from that same culture: this made it clear that human nature does not change very much, in that women have always wanted to wear beautiful things. From earliest times there is strong evidence to show that men and women were basically the same as they are today.

## A Golden Helmet — Made on Earth

Wilson then showed a beautiful golden helmet from that same city of Ur, and he commented:

"Mr. von Daniken, I wish you were down in the audience able to see this — it's very hard to see from up here (on the platform). Here is a helmet — it is a helmet of a prince who is known. It's a magnificent piece of work. It is solid gold. It is one-sixteenth of an inch in thickness — it is a helmet of a prince named Prince Meskalamdug and he lived at approximately 2,500 B.C. That is his ceremonial helmet. The holes around the side we believe were used for lacing it across his face. It is a magnificent helmet, and there it is, in this very early civilization." (It did not belong to an astronaut!)

Wilson then showed Meskalamdug's ceremonial dagger, and drew attention to the beautiful gold filigree work. It is the sort of production that anybody working today would be proud to have produced. It rivals the excellent work of Chinese craftsmen in some of the Pacific islands, experts today in filigree work. Meskalamdug's piece is every bit as good, and it dates back four and a half thousand years ago.

Those same people could build that magnificent ziggurat (a high temple tower stretching into the sky). That is the sort of construction these people were capable of, soon after we find them in their settled civilizations.

## Tunnels and Astronauts

Erich von Daniken talks about some tunnels at Tiahuanaco (in *Gods From Outer Space*). Wilson then showed a picture of a tunnel beneath the ancient city of Megiddo in Israel, cut through the solid rock. It was a magnificent structure, and the ancient Canaanite people had to use primitive tools as they cut through the rock.

These people had a magnificent capacity. We know much about them: we have historical writings about them and there is no great problem about knowing these things.

They had advanced technology way beyond what people thought they would have, before the excavations of this century.

Hezekiah's tunnel under Jerusalem is another example of the remarkable engineering feats the ancient people could undertake. That tunnel was about 1700 feet long, and an inscription was found telling how the workmen came together from opposite ends. Despite the curves they had to work through beneath the contours of the city, they met each other eventually, within about a meter.

These are remarkable achievements, and they are recorded in history. There was no astronaut help. These are simply the great constructions of men who knew what they were doing. They had advanced knowledge of engineering, way ahead of what we would have expected. Such constructions are found in all sorts of places in the ancient world.

## Alexander's Causeway at Tyre

Another good example of the effective engineering feats of ancient people was that of Alexander the Great, and the causeway he built from the mainland city of Tyre out to the island. He took the ruins of the mainland city, destroyed over 200 years earlier by Nebuchadnezzar of Babylon, and built a great causeway. It stretched half a mile from the mainland to the island where the people had fled and built a new city. Before very long there was no longer an island, for the mainland was connected to that island by the causeway.

This is one of the facts of history. If you go there today, there is no longer an island, but it is connected by a causeway to the mainland. Some of the things that Alexander the Great built in other countries were also staggering and he did not use astronauts at all!

The Romans thought so much of the achievements of Alexander the Great that right there, on that causeway at Tyre, they built an archway and called it Alexander's Arch. It is a recognition of the greatness of this man who could undertake such a remarkable engineering work. He made that causeway like the top of a rock, as a Bible prophecy had said would take place, and Alexander's chariots of war could be driven across it. He conquered those people who had been on the island.

**The Parthenon . . . the Forum . . . and Under the Earth**

There are many other achievements of the Greek period which we look back on, and recognize they were wonderful engineering achievements. The Parthenon at Athens (pictured) is one such, and the more we consider these things the more we realize that ancient people had a tremendous capacity — they had intelligence, technology, ingenuity and methodology.

The Forum at Rome is another such building. There were remarkable achievements with such buildings, as in the lifting of the great stones. In this and other buildings there were often stones bigger than some of those in the pyramids. Many of the great stones in the Western (or "Wailing") Wall in Jerusalem are bigger than the average size stones in the pyramids. And they did not use astronauts in their construction.

The same story of man's intelligence can be seen as we go down into the earth, as well as looking at constructions such as the Parthenon and the Colosseum towering into the sky. We illustrate this by pictures of Gezer in Israel (where Wilson was at one time an area supervisor in the excavation). At Gezer a Solomonic gateway was found, and also sentry-rooms alongside the main gateway. At two other sites (Megiddo and Hazor) identical patterns were found.

One of the greats of archaeology, Professor Yigael Yadin, came to Gezer and took measurements. He compared these with the excavations he had supervised at Megiddo, and found that they agreed. He then marked out a pattern at Hazor and, based on what had been found at Gezer and Megiddo, he instructed the workmen where to dig at Hazor. Where he had laid out that pattern, they found the structures he expected. It seems that the Biblical Solomon had some sort of a blueprint, and used the same pattern for a series of buildings at different cities.

The fact is, these ancient people had all sorts of ability and know-how, way ahead of what we would have expected when the modern science of archaeology began to come into its own.

### Solomon's Smelting Works and Erich von Daniken

Wilson showed slides of the general area of Ezion Geber, where Solomon had smelting works. He said that in fairness to one of his former colleagues, Professor Nelson Glueck, it was relevant to explain something. Professor Glueck had suggested that here Solomon had his furnaces, and was able to take advantage of the prevailing north wind for the furnaces at his smelting works. Professor Glueck put that theory out, but eventually he had to acknowledge that he was wrong. What he had thought was an area of furnaces was in fact a storehouse, and the cedar beams in the roof had been burnt through, causing holes. It was nothing to do with a furnace.

Such a mistake is quite understandable, for until an area has been properly excavated we do not really know what is there, and it is legitimate to put out a hypothesis. If a hypothesis is proved to be wrong, then you must be big enough to acknowledge it. Before Professor Glueck died not very long ago he was big enough to say, "I was wrong in that particular reconstruction."

The point is, archaeologists do not always simply cement down their points of view and refuse to change. (This being a reference to Erich von Daniken's statement to this effect in *Chariots Of The Gods?*.) In his writing von Daniken had actually referred to Professor Glueck's findings as an evidence of fantastic achievements of the past, but apparently had not known that Glueck had himself acknowledged his error at this point.

"I could tell you of others, such as the late G. Ernest Wright of Harvard, who likewise have made their acknowledgments to the effect that some of their hypotheses were wrong," Wilson added. (This was a reference to the fact that von Daniken claims that archaeologists are not prepared to change their point of view.)

### Art and Medicine in the Ancient World

Some of the artefacts found in ancient civilizations were beautiful pieces. Wilson showed a Roman tear bottle, as an illustration of the delicate pieces that could be made at that particular period. They were used to show a person's sorrow — his tears would be sealed in a bottle, and buried with the person who had died.

Wilson then showed a slide with various medical instruments of ancient times, and he referred to von Daniken's earlier statement that he believed that a picture from ancient times showed an early heart transplant. Wilson commented:

"We have talked about medicine and a heart transplant. Frankly, I don't believe that it was a heart transplant that Mr. von Daniken showed us on the screen,
but it was an interesting picture. I have no doubt whatever that there were interesting medical cases, and there
were some amazing operations, such as skull operations.
We know that from some of the pictures.

(We elaborate this in the later Questions and
Answers section.)

"However, we must not forget that they had all
sorts of advanced technology. As you look at some of
the medical instruments pictured on the screen I think
you are probably surprised. They are thousands of years
old. You would perhaps rather have your appendix
taken out with a modern surgical knife, but nevertheless
what they had in ancient times is staggering.

"We must forget this idea that ancient people were
primitive — with no ability. They had plenty of ability.
They could build their great amphitheaters, such as
this magnificent structure at Caesarea on the Mediterranean coast. They could build this great fortress on
Massada, 1500 feet up the mountain at the southern end
of the Dead Sea. We are not surprised to find buildings
and so much more high up on that mountain, because
men were intelligent, and had technological skills and
ingenuity from way back."

## The Pyramids of Egypt

Wilson then elaborated some of the arguments in
von Daniken's books, starting with the pyramids. Wilson
acknowledged their greatness, and the tremendous technological skill demonstrated. However, he showed that
some details of these constructions were known in history, commencing with the mastabas (stone burial
mounds) which preceded the first pyramid, the so-called
Step Pyramid of Pharaoh Zozer.

He pointed out that the pyramids could be dated
in time, that the heave-ho method was effective, that
ropes were plentiful, that the picture in the tomb of
Djehutihotep showed that a statue carved out of one
piece of stone could be as heavy as 60 tons, that it could
be pulled by ropes with the statue itself on a wooden
sled, that there was plenty of evidence to show that
Pharaohs imported great quantities of wood, and that

on some of the pyramids themselves there were dating points. These made it possible to compare how long it would take for various pyramids to be built. The evidence would suggest that it would take between 10 and 15 years to build the Great Pyramid. Pyramids were burial places for the Pharaohs and noble people.

## The Pyramids were Burial Sites
### (on the West Side of the Nile)

"In the eighty or so pyramids that have been uncovered in Egypt, about 40 mummies have been found — they never find any daddies; it is always mummies."

The pyramids were not built by astronauts. The history of the pyramids can be studied, dating from that of Pharaoh Zozer about 2,600 B.C. There are some interesting developments in construction, such as that of the Bent Pyramid that changed its angle as it was being built. These things demonstrate that clearly there is a human element involved.

"There is even an element of mistake, for one of the pyramids collapsed, in the middle of it being constructed. This indicates that these were not built by astronauts. The builders were very human, and they were associated with a new science in the building of these pyramids."

That statue pictured in Djehutihotep's tomb was 60 tons in weight, and so it was several times larger than any of the stones in the Great Pyramid. It was depicted as being hauled by 172 men. No astronaut power was necessary!

## 600 Years to Build the Great Pyramid?
## — Nonsense!

It certainly did not require some 600 years to build the Great Pyramid, as is demanded in *Chariots Of The Gods?* It took just a few years. Herodotus, the Greek historian, said it took 20 years to build the Pyramid, and 10 years to build a causeway. Even that is probably exaggerated by people who lived in the area. When he visited there it was long after the pyramids had actually been built.

—Drawing by Debra Wilson

The Egyptians learned important lessons from the collapse of this pyramid at Meidum — a very un-astronaut-like mistake. Dating points were found on some of the collapsed stones.

—Drawing by Debra Wilson

This "Bent Pyramid" of Dahshur suggests a very human adjustment, probably after the collapse of the Pyramid of Meidum. This Pyramid at Dahshur had a date on the north-eastern corner stone, saying it was laid in the 21st year of Pharaoh Seneferu (Cheop's father). About half-way up there is another date, in the same Pharaoh's 22nd year. This Pyramid is about two-thirds the size of the Great Pyramid. Clearly, 664 years were NOT required for its building!

## A STATUE MANY TIMES LARGER THAN THE
## PYRAMID STONES

—Drawing by Debra Wilson

Part of the statue scene in the tomb of Djehutihotep. An inscription stated it was 60 tons in weight and 172 men are shown hauling it by ropes, on a wooden sled.

# Chapter 4:

## WILSON'S CHALLENGE: Part 2 — SOME OF VON DANIKEN'S FAVORITES

IN THE SECOND HALF OF HIS ADDRESS WILSON DEALT MORE SPECIFICALLY WITH TOPICS OFTEN REFERRED TO BY VON DANIKEN . . .

### The Nazca Plain

Another area of interest is that of the Nazca Plain. Etched into those Plains are monkeys and other figures which have humanistic and religious overtones, for these people worshipped both the stars and the plants. I have had long conversations with a missionary friend (Reverend Donald Bond) who has lived in Peru for some 17 years. At the time when I was speaking to him he was on leave from Nazca where he actually lives.

"Mr. von Daniken's pictures suggest astronauts landing on this Plain, and tonight we have heard some very interesting variations of that earlier theme." (It is a problem in many areas with Mr. von Daniken to pin him down as to what he actually means.) "His earlier pictures certainly seem to suggest that he thought that the whole of the Nazca Plain was a great airfield, but now he appears to be talking about selected areas only. He does not easily give up particular theories!"

Wilson showed a picture of someone standing on the Nazca lines, and this made it clear that most of the lines were very narrow, being only between four and six inches across. Those lines were about one inch deep.

"Some of the lines are larger, but those that run for great distances are just a few inches, as the measure against the line shows. The measure shows that they range from four to six inches across, and of course these could not be the landing strips of aircraft — unless they were very tiny, little aircraft!

"Nor could the outlines that are there represent giant parking bays for aircraft. They simply are not big enough. Some lines run into each other, while others depict various kinds of birds and animals, such as the humming bird figure."

Wilson showed a picture of Reverend Donald Bond pointing to some of the figures, making it clear that they simply could not be an area such as a parking bay for the landing of aircraft in ancient times. The so-called "parking bays" are in fact only a few feet across.

The German scientist Maria Reiche has investigated these lines at great length, and she believes that they are an astronomical calendar. Many of them point to the rising points of various stars, and are associated with such heavenly phenomena as the equinoxes, and the points of the solstices. It is possible to follow the path of the sun every two months along different lines. They appear to be associated with the heavens.

Apart from such a construction it is difficult to interpret them, for in the main they are lines that appear to start from nowhere and go to nowhere. We saw that many of them are in circles, or in patterns of lines that run into each other, like a never-ending maze. It is true that we do not know all the explanation, but it is certainly true that these lines are nothing to do with landing strips, or parking bays for aircraft in ancient times.

### The Palenque Astronaut

At this point Wilson showed the picture of the Palenque "astronaut," which von Daniken, in *Chariots Of The Gods?*, identified as possibly being the god Kukulkan.

"Mr. von Daniken tonight has talked about this particular picture. He chose this particular man, but we know when he was there. It comes from Palenque, and details are on his sarcophagus, his tomb. There he is shown, in Mr. von Daniken's own picture, without a tunic, and without anything on his legs, though he has serpents coming out from his head, and there are other serpents higher in the picture, and so you can go on.

"Here is another picture of the same man, but this time it is taken from the *National Geographic* magazine, and it is clearer than the one I have just shown you. Now you can see the man seated. His head is clearly shown, and it is also clear that he had a club foot. Indeed, the archaeologist who went and examined this sarcophagus soon after it had been found, was himself born with a club foot — the same type of deformity

**THE RULER PACAL . . . between symbols of Heaven and Earth. Thus it is fitting for him to be shown being carried on a Mayan throne chair and (probably) eating fruit as he journeys.**
—Drawing by Debra Wilson

On top is a bird symbolizing heaven . . . a cross-shaped device which is the Mayan tree supporting heaven, and below is a grotesque earth monster, symbol of the underworld. These same symbols are often found in other Mayan art. — Graham Massey, in "The Case of the Ancient Astronauts."

shown in this figure. That was an interesting coincidence, and it is written up in the journals as to how the archaeologist and a man with him discussed this particular thing. We can count the man's toes. If he was going to shoot off into space with bare feet, he was rather foolish!

"He would have needed some sort of helmet, but we find that his head is outside the so-called space ship. The fact is, it is a ruler seated on his throne. You can actually trace the arms, and the back of the throne, and underneath you can see depicted the monster of the underworld carved into that seat. It is nothing more than a throne chair.

It is showing this man Pacal at the time of his death, and the date is actually given on the sarcophagus — it is just before 700 A.D. If we are to accept that this is anything to do with ancient astronauts, we have to condense all sorts of things chronologically and bring them into one particular time to suit our preconceived notions. Of course, we are not prepared to do that.

(In his own presentation Mr. von Daniken said that he had been criticized because the astronaut should be shown as turned around looking into the heavens, and he made the point that this made his own presentation even better because an astronaut was of course directed towards the heavens. However, his earlier description was that the man looked like a racing motor cyclist. He gives this in *Chariots Of The Gods?*, and he also used the same description in the earlier part of his lecture at the time of this debate. Now we find he conveniently switches, and that is typical of Mr. von Daniken. He has a great capacity to adjust an argument so that it somehow will fit his preconceived notion. "Don't confuse me with such facts," seems to be his attitude.)

### The Easter Island Statues

Wilson next discussed the Easter Island statues, using the pictures used by Thor Heyerdahl in his excellent book *Aku Aku*. Not only were there hundreds of stone statues at Easter Island, but there were also evidences from where they were constructed, and from where the stone "hats" on their top were made. Some of the ramps associated with the statues were still *in situ*, and it was these ramps that made it possible for the hats to be hauled up into position.

Wilson discussed various questions relating to the statues, and gave pictorial evidence to show how they were constructed, how they were lifted, and how they were carted across the plains, as discussed in Chapter 13 of this book.

The people of Easter Island are not primitive, and they have good farming methods. They have a rainfall of about 45 inches a year, and good crops, with such things as sweet potatoes growing very well. These people have demonstrated that they are capable of a great deal of ingenuity.

An outline of the god-figure had been flaked out of the stone by these people, by arrangement with Thor Heyerdahl, in just a few days — NOT several weeks.

After showing how the statue was lifted by a few men, Wilson made the point, "No astronauts . . . no hydraulic power . . . and after several days just two poles and a series of ropes . . . These are not astronauts depicted there. They are modern people living on Easter Island."

The Mayor of Easter Island and the men who worked with him, paid by Thor Heyerdahl, were descendants of the so-called long ears. These were earlier people who had caused their ears to grow to remarkable lengths by putting weights into the lobes of the ears. They themselves had certain traditions as to where they came from: they believe that they came from across the sea, and not from the stars as von Daniken has conjectured. Although there has been inter-mixing with the various Pacific Island peoples, the long ears traditionally came from such places as Chile, and it is at least possible that one wave of immigrants did indeed come from the South American continent.

## Conclusions from Thor Heyerdahl

Wilson pointed out that Thor Heyerdahl's experiments had shown how the statues could be chiselled out of the volcanic rock, how they could be erected, and how they could even be hauled across the plain — as demonstrated by 180 people to whom a meal was first given. After some preliminary difficulties, they eventually managed to haul one of the statues a considerable distance until they were told to stop.

"Thor Heyerdahl tells us that once it got moving, it moved across that plain as easily as though they were all pulling empty soap boxes. They didn't need astronaut power, and they didn't have any hydraulic power. They had plenty of manpower, and over and over again in ancient times the secret is just that — good, effective manpower, and ingenuity. Thus statues such as those at Easter Island could be lifted by ordinary men who happened to have the tradition passed on to them from way back."

Wilson showed another carved statue, and this time there was a three-masted ship shown on its surface. "You can see that three-masted ship carved into the statue, and as you can see from the white marks on the statue, the markings outlining the ship had been buried below the earth for a considerable period of time. These people had their own tradition of where they came from. It was not that they came from spacemen, but that they came across the sea by ship."

Thor Heyerdahl tells us, by the way, that we have a date for the construction of the last of the statues to be built. It was about 1700 A.D. (Thor Heyerdahl's date is given in Ronald Story's *Space Gods Revealed* as "about 1680 A.D.")

## The Gods of Ancient People

Wilson made a number of references to the gods of ancient people. He showed by slides that there were written records of early people, such as those from Nuzi in the general area that the patriarch Abraham of the Bible moved around. Clay gods at Nuzi were title deeds as well as being worshipped. They had practical value, but they were also linked with heavenly beings. In Ur, the city of the patriarch Abraham, the people actually worshipped many gods, but they especially worshipped Nannar the Moon God. They had a great temple tower, towering into the sky, and it was the ziggurat of Nannar.

In Egypt the Pharaoh Akhenaton came to be regarded as a heretic. Before his time there had been thousands of gods worshipped in Egypt, and after his death they reverted to that polytheism, the worship of many gods. Akhenaton made the claim that there was only the one god in the heavens, Ra the great Sun God, and himself. He claimed that he himself was the great manifestation of Ra, and that Ra was being worshipped as the people worshipped Akhenaton himself, and that nothing else could be worshipped. Akhenaton identified himself with the rays of the sun, and the idea is that Akhenaton was supposedly the manifestation of the sun god.

Over and over again we find that people thought of a power beyond themselves, and that power was very often associated with heavenly bodies.

### Mythologies Often Linked to Worship of Heavenly Bodies

This association of the gods with heavenly bodies is the answer to many of the suppositions made in Mr. von Daniken's books. Over in Egypt they worshipped many gods, and they had concepts concerning the life to come, and those point to two main things in archaeology that distinguish man from all other creatures. They are

1. that there is a god or gods, and man wants to find him; and
2. there is life beyond the grave.

At this point Dr. Wilson showed slides from the Egyptian *Book Of The Dead,* giving some of the mythological teachings concerning the judgment of the dead and the entrance into the life beyond. The gods could be hoodwinked (by paying the priests), and so a man could be conducted safely into the next stages of eternity. They could worship gods even in animal form, as shown in those same pictures from the *Book Of The Dead.* Beings that were part-animal and part-man were part of their mythology.

They also made all sorts of preparation for that life to come in which they believed.

### Did Astronauts give "a Bright Young Prince" in Egypt Embalming Secrets?

Another point relates to embalming. When a man died in ancient Egypt, if he was to be embalmed (if he could pay the price) the soft parts of his body would be taken out and they would be put in four canopic (or funerary) jars. They had symbols of some of the gods on them — the face of a man, the face of a dog, the face of a monkey, and of a hawk. The canopic jars would be put back inside the man and he would be sewn up. Then the embalming processes would take place.

Clearly this could not be related in any way to that actual body ever being reincarnated, or some such thing. The brain itself was taken out, and as far as we know that brain was never associated with the man again.

The point of this is that in *Chariots Of The Gods?* we have the possibility put forward of visitors from space telling some bright young prince in Egypt about embalming. The fact is, if the bright young prince fell for that as a means of using the same body again, he was extremely gullible. However, gullibility is not only an ancient concept!

(Many gullible people today fall for Mr. von Daniken's highly conjectural hypotheses.)

People in Egypt worshipped all sorts of objects and things, such as Hequet the frog goddess who was associated with fertility, and various beings that were part-animal and part-man. They would worship Hathor the cow goddess, having the face of a woman and the ears of a cow. Over in Canaan the god Baal was associated with the lightning and the thunder. Asherah, the goddess of sex and lust, was the bride of Baal, and also of Baal's father El.

Ancient people made images of their god or gods, and over and over again those gods are associated with the heavens — with the sun, and the moon and the stars. Sometimes they are known by different names, as with the moon god being Ulumq over in Marib. That was the capital of Sheba, where the Queen of Sheba came from, as recorded in the First Book of Kings in the Bible.

Similarly Diana of the Ephesians, the many-breasted figure that supposedly fell from the heavens, is also associated with the heavens. Consistently, these ancient gods are often so associated.

Not only did early people worship the gods of the heavens, but over and over again they record their activities. Thus we are able to compare the ancient records of their religious activities, their commercial activities, their rebellions against their overlords, their conquests in war — and their service to the gods. There is considerable similarity to the activities of ordinary human beings today.

## DIANA OF THE EPHESIANS
The many-breasted goddess that supposedly fell from heaven in
this form.  Many ancient peoples worshipped the sun, the moon,
and the stars, and had myths of beings that came down from
the skies.

—Drawing by Debra Wilson

## Von Daniken and "Plural Gods" in the Old Testament

In passing it is relevant to mention that the word "El" has the same root as "Elohim" in the Bible. When we read "Elohim bara" in Genesis Chapter 1, that is merely the plural form of "God." Sometimes it is known as "the royal plural," and it shows the concept of the God-head acting in unison. It is a plural word, "Elohim," with a singular verb, "bara" — "The Gods, He created." The concept of the God-head being plural is implied in that first verse in Genesis, with that usage of the royal plural.

"The Bible records are especially reliable documents — we are constantly impressed with those Bible writers, as shown by the evidence from archaeology. The Bible Books were written by those who were actually there.

"Mr. von Daniken's theories over and over again touch theology. And I find it interesting that in many ways these ancient people (who were neighbors of the Hebrews) talked about things, and wrote about things, that looked on to days to come. . . . Many of the written records actually touched incidents of the Bible, both Old and New Testaments alike. . . ."

## Man was Intelligent — but had no Astronaut Help!

"The more we study these ancient records on stones, on pieces of leather, on wood, on papyrus, in clay, or whatever, we find that the stones cry out. And, ladies and gentlemen, they do not cry out to tell us that we ever came from astronauts from outer space. They tell us that right from early times man was intelligent, man was ingenious, man is a product of this very culture of which we today are a part.

"As a practising Christian, I come ultimately to the statement in the Bible itself, that man was made in the image of the One True God, the God of Heaven.

"Thank you, ladies and gentlemen."

# Chapter 5:

## REBUTTAL BY
## ERICH VON DANIKEN

(We make it clear again that we cannot give a verbatim report of Mr. von Daniken's rebuttal, by the stipulation already referred to.)

### An Airplane and Nazca

Mr. von Daniken stated that he did not see the relevance to his own theory of much of Dr. Wilson's "wonderful lecture." However, he had made notes and would explain some things as he saw them. He started first with a further explanation concerning the lines on the Plain of Nazca. He claimed that he had shown a slide that had a large line on it, and not just lines of a few inches, because those small lines of only a few inches were something completely different. If an aeroplane had come from the skies and landed on the Nazca Plain, surely it would leave lines behind. Even a jeep driven across there today leaves impressions behind.

In usual von Daniken style he suggests, "Let us assume that the inhabitants were watching the doings" as the spacecraft landed. We have that "let us assume" approach so often in Mr. von Daniken's writings, and we found it again at the time of this debate!

After the gods had gone away we are told that the natives come out from their hiding place. They look at the two lines left there, in astonishment: those two lines were a landing track and a take-off track. (With the wind and against the wind? Why not just one landing and take-off strip?)

Mr. von Daniken tells us, "The lines became holy — they have to do with the gods, and so they are perfected and kept in order." The natives completed them and kept them in good order, and hoped for the gods to return.

As time went by and the gods did not return, the natives completed more lines. They extended north, south, east and west — large, thin, long lines, all being for the gods. Much later, a priest comes to the conclusion that offerings should be made to the gods, and so, many generations later, they begin to carve figures like birds, animals, spiders and fruit, but of such a nature that they can only be seen by beings flying from a very great height.

"That is my explanation about the Plain of Nazca, and I admit that this explanation is a speculation, but a justifiable one." Mr. von Daniken said that all the other interpretations that had been made about the Plain of Nazca were also speculations.

Mr. von Daniken acknowledged that there were indeed records from the past, but that they had not always been interpreted as they should be.

### The Astronauts Would have left Tools

Mr. von Daniken referred to the fact that Dr. Wilson had shown evidence from archaeology around the world, and had stated that these great buildings had not been built by astronauts. Mr. von Daniken quite agreed, but he was referring to something else. Quite often when natives were used in construction activities they were given gifts such as beads or mirrors, or useful things such as tools, knives, hatchets and pots. This was done when it was necessary to gain the favor of those local people. It is therefore reasonable to believe that some of the astronauts would have left our forefathers some tools.

(One problem is that the tools left lying around in the areas claimed by Mr. von Daniken to be associated with astronauts, are over and over again very primitive, and they involve materials known at various places around the earth. For instance, the flint stones on Easter Island were very much a product of Easter Island, as also were those left lying near the great stone that was not completed at Baal-Bek in Lebanon.)

Mr. von Daniken himself went on to say that until now no one has ever found any of the tools left on earth from an extra-terrestrial visit. If we are to look for such objects on our beautiful blue planet we would not look at the ice caps of the North and South Pole, nor would we look in any of the great areas of desert. If then you take away the gigantic forests such as those in Central America and South America, the surface has again become smaller. The biggest part of the globe is water, and nothing would ever be found there either.

"Even if I speculate — and I make a crazy speculation — that these spacemen should have left a gigantic object here," it is still probable that we would not see such an object.   When the pyramids in Central America were discovered, they had been completely covered by the surrounding jungle.   If a big object was in fact left in such an area, in fifty years it would be completely covered by encroaching growth, and 200 years later there would be trees all around it.   Perhaps there would even be a large hill covering it in some people's back yard!

### The Pyramids — One Stone Every Two Minutes?

In relation to the pyramids in Egypt, Mr. von Daniken acknowledged that there was a lot of controversy going on, but then he stated, "I never said that extra-terrestrials constructed the pyramids, but in fact I have speculated that our ancestors had a knowledge or some tool, or maybe both, which helped them to make such gigantic constructions in antiquity."

(He also speculated, in *Chariots Of The Gods?*, it would take 664 years to build the Great Pyramid, and gave "evidence" to indicate they were beyond human ability.)

Mr. von Daniken went on to say that he had made certain calculations based on the archaeological claims that the Great Pyramid was constructed in about twenty years.   Archaeologists say that there are about two and a half million blocks in the pyramids, with an average size of about two and a half tons.   If two and a half million blocks are divided by twenty years, that means that every year about 120,000 blocks would be built into the Great Pyramid.   If we took 300 working days in a year, and each working day had 13 hours, they would have to cut one stone out of the rock and put it in its place and polish it, at the rate of one every two minutes.

(Mr. von Daniken's theories are interesting, but what he does not include in his statement is the possibility that very large numbers of workmen were employed.   The Greek historian Herodotus suggests that 100,000 men at a time were employed.   Now let us have another look at von Daniken's figures.   On his own calculations, there would have been one block every two minutes.   That is 30 in an hour, 390 in a day, 117,000 in a year, and then two million three hundred and forty thousand in 20 years. If Herodotus is correct (and von Daniken is using his figure to show how ridiculous it is to think that men could build this structure in 20 years) then 100,000 men would complete all that was involved with 117,000 stones each year. That is to say, each individual man completed just a fraction over one stone in a whole year of 300 working days. He would need team-work of course — such as 20 men completing everything involved with 24 stones each year. Clearly it is not so unlikely after all!)

(Let us be prepared to cut the figure given by Herodotus by a factor of five, and so bring the men down to 20,000. Now we have each man cutting and being responsible for five stones per year. Either way it certainly becomes obvious that we do not need more than 600 years, which von Daniken claimed. It is his figure that becomes nonsensical, and not that of Herodotus, or of the archaeologists whom he tends to deride so often in *Chariots Of The Gods?* and in the debate at North Dakota.)

### No Translation About the Palenque "Astronaut"?

Mr. von Daniken claimed that until the present time we have not been able to have a translation of the inscriptions around the figure at Palenque. However, he went on to acknowledge that some parts of it seemed to be translatable.

He claimed that in all the Maya culture they had never found a figure sitting in that pose. (*Some Trust In Chariots* depicts a rather similar figure, and there are others. Reverend Donald Bond, mentioned earlier in this book, has been a missionary in Peru for 17 years. He was impressed with the likeness of this figure to other figures now known, showing rulers being carried across great distances by slaves. Part of the glyphs on that sarcophagus have been interpreted: they tell us that this man's name was Pacal, and that he died in the last part of the 7th Century A.D.

### Now the Easter Island Statues were NOT made by Extra-terrestrials!

Mr. von Daniken went on to refer to the Easter Island statues. He said it was never his opinion, and he has never published it, that the statues were made by extra-terrestrials.

(After showing that people of antiquity could not, in his opinion, have built them, Mr. von Daniken asks a series of questions, "Then who cut the statues out of the rock, who carved them and transported them to their sites?" etc., etc., etc., *Chariots Of The Gods?*, page 91.)

(We stress that both *Chariots Of The Gods?* and *Gods From Outer Space* have his "visitors hypothesis" to explain the construction of the statues. Now apparently the "visitors" were from somewhere else, and not from his consistently conjectured space stations.)

"I speculate again that there was an unknown tool," he said at North Dakota. With that tool some priests were able to make some statues in a very easy way. One day the tools broke, and the visitors had long gone, and could not be asked for help, so the priests asked the people to help them. Thus it was that "now night and day, for weeks and months, they chiselled with primitive stone chisels on the rock."

Mr. von Daniken referred to Thor Heyerdahl's explanation — that hundreds of tools had been found, and so that was the way the statues had been made. Von Daniken suggested that an opposite conclusion was possible, that because the tools were lying around and many statues were unfinished, this indicated that the tools were not satisfactory for the work. Otherwise, why were not the statues completed? He claims that the people realized it was not possible to complete the work with these primitive tools, and so they gave up. That is why the chisels were found, and not the other way around.

(There are, of course, other possible explanations as to why a people would not complete a difficult task, but von Daniken has the remarkable knack of finding astronauts as the answer to any problem that appears to be at all difficult. Thor Heyerdahl's experiments showed clearly that the stone flints could be effective in chiselling the statues out of the volcanic rock, and that statues were still being erected about 300 years ago.)

(Von Daniken's statement that Thor Heyerdahl's men had lifted only the smallest statue on the island is clearly open to challenge. Heyerdahl's own statement is that it was a statue about 25 to 30 tons in weight, which puts it in the medium bracket of the statues on the island. It was not the smallest statue as von Daniken claimed.)

—Drawing by Debra Wilson
**The Mayor of Easter Island with several other men demonstrated
how a statue could be raised.  Poles, ropes and stones were used.
No hydraulic power, and no astronauts!**

### Visits by Alien Astronauts Should be Considered

Mr. von Daniken claimed that scientists should be
prepared to get to the truth, but it was not possible
to do this if one started out with fixed and allegedly
unassailable positions.  Very often positions maintained
in textbooks are accepted as though they are proved.
Then they are maintained as dogma, but very often the
work of scholars is based on that of their predecessors,
and that does not include the possibility of visits by alien
astronauts (such as at Easter Island — see above *re* von
Daniken's own rejection of astronauts visiting Easter
Island!)

In their working hypotheses, according to von Daniken, the actual achievement of space travel in earlier
times was beyond the bounds of their conception.  Scientific proofs of today are being confused with yesterday's
arguments in our approach to the study of the science of
the future.

## Rock and Cave Drawings

Mr. von Daniken also referred to rock and cave drawings around the world which are very often interpreted as being associated with myths and hunting legends. That is a very respectable solution provided other possibilities can be excluded. It should be recognized that cave dwellers might have seen alien astronauts, and that this was the real reason for certain representations in their art. Such an explanation is rejected by many scholars on the grounds that there were no alien cosmonauts.

"But why not? Where is the scientific proof? It would be fairer to respect the situations that it cannot be proved that our rock paintings were not influenced by alien cosmonauts. Nor can it be proved that the drawings were ritual or hunting magic."

(In Chapter 9 we discuss some of the cave drawings by Australian Aborigines. They were usually drawn on rocks in the open, or not far inside caves. They were subject to weathering and the effects of the atmosphere. Over and over again they fade, and many have disappeared. Some have been regularly touched up by authorized tribespeople. Some have even been drawn this century. Others depict early European visitors, less than 200 years ago. Others again clearly show hunting and mythical scenes, with a folk-lore or religious significance. The drawings are not always exact or to scale — and neither are the Wandjina figures in the Kimberleys, to which von Daniken refers. The same art style is used in both hunting and mythological representations. "Antennae" and coloration is remarkably similar to hair styles and body paintings still used on ceremonial occasions by Aborigines in the area today. They have their sagas and traditions, and these include stories about the stars, as in cultures around the world.)

(All people, including children, wonder about the moon and the stars. Nursery rhymes and myths sometimes have much in common, in pointing to the human interest and questioning about the vastness of the universe by which we are surrounded.)

**Chapter 6:**

# REBUTTAL BY CLIFFORD WILSON

[Note: This has been legitimately edited for literary style, but is almost entirely a verbatim transcript. It is relevant to add that the agreed arrangement as to the debate format was not strictly adhered to, partly because of technical problems. Thus the second rebuttal period was omitted. However, the question and answer period made up for this to some extent.

[In addition, a large number of written questions were handed in and these are answered in Chapters 8 to 16 of this book. They deal further with a number of interesting topics such as heart transplants, the virtually invisible Sirius B star, and von Daniken's supposedly "pure" case of the visitor in a straw suit.]

Thank you, Mr. von Daniken, for those comments.

I gathered at the beginning you were asking, "What has my presentation got to do with your books?" Well, we are not actually debating your books: we are debating the question, "Does the historical and archaeological evidence support the proposition that ancient human civilization was influenced by astronauts from outer space?" I am quite convinced that all that I said (and others who talked to me in the interval were convinced) was very much related to the topic to be debated.

The only criticism that came to me in that time actually was, "Didn't I refer too much to Mr. von Daniken's books?" I referred to his books in considerable detail in all sorts of ways, and I would be very happy to refer to them very much more, but I felt that I should not do that.

### "Gods in their Own Image"

There is so much I should like to answer that in 15 minutes I am going to find it very difficult. However, let us pick some points here and there. First of all, let us look at the approach concerning the gods in their own image. It is true that there is this concept of "in their own image," but there are also various distortions of actual records that are in the Bible.

One significant clue to many of these records is to go back to the Bible. I am not going to give a Bible lecture, but Erich von Daniken and myself are agreed that much that he has to say is touching the realm of theology. Over and over again as you compare the Bible records with those of the Babylonians and others, these last are distortions.

Let me give you one example. Mr. von Daniken himself refers to the Babylonian *Epic of Gilgamesh.* If I may say so, he makes some quite serious errors of chronology in relation to that Epic. He conjectures that the *Epic of Gilgamesh* came from a Latin-American culture, finding its way over into Egypt, and then getting into the hands of Moses and so it became the basis for the Book of Genesis and perhaps even the Book of Exodus!!

In that he has some quite serious *non sequiturs* (illogical conclusions not justified by the evidence).

However, the point I want to make is this: That *Epic of Gilgamesh,* which includes the Babylonian story of the flood, has the Babylonian Noah coming out from his vessel after the flood, making a sacrifice to the gods, and then the gods coming like a swarm of flies to partake of that sacrifice. You see, the poor gods had not been fed while the flood was on, and man was not there to feed them. They had objected to the fact that man's snoring awoke them, and they objected to the fact that some of the gods had done this foolish thing of bringing on a flood — why did they not just let wild animals loose to slay some of the humans? . . . and so on.

I want to make the point very strongly, and I make it very sincerely as an academic, that very often these records of the past are distortions and grotesque absurdities. I am not talking about Mr. von Daniken's books, but about the Babylonian records and also about other records that touch the Bible, and can be compared with the Bible records. Over and over again the Bible records are remarkably accurate and those others are distorted.

## The Incas and Hot-air Balloons

Let us go on to some other things. Mr. von Daniken has an interesting style. "Did I claim Incas had no hot air balloons?" he asks, and later he says, "Let us speculate," and he keeps on with that sort of approach. "Let us suppose we were living 500 years in the past," "Let us play a little game here together." I find this very interesting! He suggests to us, "Let us use our imagination once more . . ." As I say, this is an interesting approach, but it is NOT a scientific approach.

. . . . . . . . . .

> "Von Daniken is part of a growing movement of irrationalism that more often than not attacks established knowledge with a great deal of verve but little solid evidence. It is too popular to be simply ignored or laughed at, and too important, because any move away from real knowledge can be dangerous." — Graham Massey, "The Case of the Ancient Astronauts."

. . . . . . . . . .

Unfortunately a great deal we have heard in this debate is of this nature, and the same is often true throughout Mr. von Daniken's books. He takes these apparently interesting and plausible suggestions, and then from those he goes on and makes quite definite conclusions, as though the case has been established. The fact is, at point after point that simply is not so, and the case has NOT been established. His use of such expressions might sound convincing, but at times it is even irrelevant.

For instance, as for the matter of "Did I say that Incas had no hot air balloons?" The fact is, I did not say that he did! Anyway, did those hot air balloons need the runways that Mr. von Daniken tells us were there as runways on the Nazca Plain?

My point is there is something wrong somewhere. As far as I know, balloons (and vehicles from space) come down and they just land. They do not need runways. No one is challenging the fact that these priests of ancient times had this capacity to go up in air balloons. They go UP in air balloons. The type of material of which those air balloons had been made has been found, and it is indeed true that an experiment was made from the earth. But these were NOT beings coming down from space. As I say, we do not need runways for such vehicles.

### That "Astronaut" at Palenque

In the matter of the man depicted on the sarcophagus at Palenque in Mexico, the astronaut-type figure: first let me say that there ARE other similar pictures in the general areas of Latin and South America. They depict this sort of person actually being carried across the roads. They did not have wheeled vehicles, and there are pictures of rulers being carried. When someone is carried along like this, for perhaps ten or fifteen miles, it becomes very uncomfortable.

Mr. von Daniken wants us to believe that it is reasonable to make the assumption that he makes, because we do not have all of the translation from that particular sarcophagus, but we have enough translation to know two important things. One is that the man was a ruler named Pacal, and that he lived and died in the seventh century A.D. That is only one of the many things we could talk about with this picture. Another is the date it was found — it was 1952, and not 1935 as Mr. von Daniken mentions in his book. My point in rebuttal is that we have enough information to show that this is something actually set in solid history.

I agree with some of the things that Mr. von Daniken said, such as when he asked, "Is it such a crime to interpret?" and so on. However, I am not saying it is a crime, and I would agree that it is INTERESTING to do this, SO LONG as it is clear that it is SPECULATION and is not put out as though it is something to be taken ultra-seriously.

### God with Smoke . . . Fire . . . and Noise

Let us go on. Mr. von Daniken makes the point that the so-called Almighty God is always associated with smoke, with fire, with loud noise, whenever He descends, and so on. It would be a long theological debate to start on that, but it just is not true. It is his argument — not mine. He is making the point of how God appears. He quietly walks in the Garden of Eden in the very first story we have of this God of the Bible.

I could tell you more about this matter of God revealing Himself to men: it simply is not true that the God of the Bible is always associated with great, loud noises. The picture of God in the Bible is one of consistency.

### "I Saw Visions of God" — Omitted by von Daniken

I brought a Bible with me tonight, in case it was quoted. Mr. von Daniken does us a disservice when he

quotes Ezekiel as he did.   Dr. Blumrich is rationalizing
in an extreme way to quote another writer when he
makes his interpretation of Ezekiel's supposed space-ship,
and Mr. von Daniken himself does not quote several
words in his book *Chariots Of The Gods?*, and again in
this debate he did not quote those words again.   It could
be argued that that was his prerogative — that it was
not in his particular interest to go back and give the
very beginning of the story.   But there in Ezekiel Chapter
1 that Mr. von Daniken read from, Ezekiel actually says
that HE SAW VISIONS OF GOD.   HE STATES VERY
CLEARLY, RIGHT AT THE BEGINNING, THAT IT IS A
VISION.

Mr. von Daniken omitted the words "I saw visions
of God."   Now if it is a vision, it certainly is not some
physical machine, and there is not really any need to
discuss this particular point any further.   Some of the
audience would know of Barry Downing, who wrote
a book with a title something like *U.F.O.s And The Bible*.
It is relevant, and I quote him, not because I agree with
him at every point, for I do not.   He is a friend, but I am
making the point that he sees U.F.O.s as being in use at
various points through the Bible, and I do not.

Barry Downing himself makes the point that we do
not need to discuss this matter of Ezekiel, because he
says straight-out that it is a vision.   So it is that,
although we saw and heard much about this from Mr.
von Daniken tonight, it really is a hot air thing.   If
Ezekiel says it was a vision, it was not a literal vehicle
at all.

### Legends in Fiji . . . Australia . . . and Africa

Let us go on.   Let us take this concept of these
jungle people with their language, and their stories of
the gods visiting them.   I have lived in Fiji.   I could tell
you stories of the myths and traditions of these people.
One is concerning anyone who did not pay their respects
to the shark god — and so their children would be born
with the face of a shark; and there is a great deal of
that sort of thing, but you never actually see the shark
people themselves.   You never see these things they say
are there in their midst.   People do have such myths
and distortions, and over and over again they are simply
demonstrating a good imagination.

Or take these things we heard about from Australia,

my own home country. There is a very good book written recently by Dr. Peter White of Sydney University, and it is called *The Past Is Human*. I do not think it is over here in the U.S. yet — it is published by Angus & Robertson, Sydney, Australia. Dr. White goes into great depth about some of these things relating to the Australian Aboriginal rock paintings.

The fact is that those paintings are consistently touched up by the Aboriginal people. They are colored, and they would not last unless they WERE touched up. They are consistently added to, and those cave paintings are not ancient things revealing information about space visits at all. They are part of the Aborigines' present-day mythology, the same as so many people have around the world.

Time is beating me, but let us consider some of these things about the Sirius system. Mr. von Daniken has given us a whole lot of interesting information about Sirius, and about new things we perhaps have not known about. If the facts are eventually shown to be correct it may very well be in the category of the Barney and Betty Hill situation where details about a certain star were given at the time of their contact with a U.F.O. entity. That information was not known by scholars until some considerable period later. This touches another area, and perhaps Erich von Daniken and I on another occasion will debate how U.F.O's and these beings that occupy them can give their messages. They do give messages sometimes — I fully accept that, but they do not come from outer space.

(This matter of the Sirius B star is discussed further in the later section dealing with answers to questions.)

### Life in Space?

There are many other points. Do these extra-terrestrials really exist? Mr. von Daniken says yes — "Science says there is life out there." That gets very close to the whole subject of the debate tonight. He has made a very definite statement, that science says "Yes, there is life out there." I want to say in all seriousness that science cannot say that as an actual established fact, because there is no certain knowledge of one single planet outside our solar system.

When I found this out I was astounded. We elaborate
it in a chapter of *Crash Go The Chariots*. It was information given to me by the late Professor Fred Giles, Jr.,
Professor of Physics and Astronomy at the University
of South Carolina where I also was on the Professorial
staff.  He made the point very strongly, but at first I
would not believe it, and so I checked with others.  I
wondered just what Dr. Giles meant.

It is indeed true that there are galaxies — there are
billions of stars out there, but I found out that it is true
no one can say for certain that one single one of them
is a planet. (Note — a planet would be "solid," not just
a gaseous body.)

You can come and debate this with me all night,
but I repeat that I am talking about certain knowledge.
All we can say ultimately is that, with all the galaxies,
probably, if you like, there is another planet or more
outside our solar system.  That would be as far as you
can go.  There is not one scintilla of truth in the statement that certainly there is life out there, or that extra-
terrestrials really exist.  That is putting the conclusion
without the evidence.

### "There is no Doubt" or "Pure Guesswork"?

On this matter, Mr. von Daniken quotes a particular
scientific conference in his book *Chariots Of The Gods?*
and I went to the trouble of getting the report of that
conference at Green Bank in Virginia.  He claimed that
"there is no doubt" about the fact of planets similar to
the earth, but the report says, "Estimation of the average
number of planets (with environments able to develop
life) . . . is a matter of pure guesswork."  "A matter
of pure guesswork."  As that report further makes clear,
we have no certain knowledge of life out there.  The
only planet about which we have any certainty (about
life) is this planet on which we live.

I think actually the major criticism I have of Mr.
von Daniken's hypothesis (and I must give it because
it is highly relevant to the subject of our debate) is this
matter of the breeding experiments.  He has talked about
these things at length tonight, and of course he does
so in his books.  The fact is, in this area I suggest Mr.
von Daniken is confusing certain relationships and terms.
It may be a matter of translation!  It may be a matter

of the English language, the American language, or the Australian language as against the Swiss.

Whatever the reason, Mr. von Daniken tends to confuse the respective roles of chromosomes and genes. They have BOTH got to match up, and it would be extremely unlikely for that to take place. If this WERE to happen it would NOT be that zombies would be transformed into geniuses. The fact is, if they WERE able to be matched up they would already be bright people. There would not be the sort of dramatic changes that Mr. von Daniken is talking about.

. . . . . . . . . .

"Mated with a human being? Why, we'd be much more likely to successfully mate with a petunia than with an extraterrestrial!" (Carl Sagan, in TV presentation "The Case of the Ancient Astronauts."

. . . . . . . . . .

### No Evidence Left by a Spacecraft

My time has gone. I simply say that the evidence I have given tonight clearly shows some of the ways in which men have been ingenious, men have been intelligent, men have had technological abilities, men have been able to do all sorts of fantastic things. There is not one bit of evidence of a spacecraft being left here, or of their tools being left behind. The tools that Mr. von Daniken talks about are primitive stone, and similar type of tool. Astronauts surely would have something far more advanced, IF we are to believe in them.

I submit, Mr. Chairman, Mr. von Daniken, ladies and gentlemen, that the historical and archaeological evidence does NOT support the proposition that ancient human civilization was influenced by astronauts from outer space.

Thank you.

. . . . . . . . . .

"Erich von Daniken — Another dabbler in economically profitable guesswork whose researches are dismissed by scientists as 'science fiction' — and cut even less ice in the s.f. (science fiction—Ed.) field itself . . . The book ("Chariots Of The Gods?—Ed.) caused a stir in the same quarters as Adamski's "Flying Saucers Have Landed" and offered us little real proof of anything." — Brian Ash, "Who's Who In Science Fiction," 1976, Sphere Books, London, pp. 197 ff.

**Chapter 7:**

# ANSWERING THE QUESTIONS AT NORTH DAKOTA

During the intermission question cards were collected from the audience at the North Dakota State University. The Moderator (Professor Jovan Brkic) had these put in two separate compartments, one for Mr. von Daniken and one for Dr. Wilson. He then selected them at random, taking one from each container and then one from the other. For each question the person addressed could have three minutes to answer, and then this could be rebutted by the other speaker, also for three minutes, if he so chose.

Once again, because of Mr. von Daniken's restriction, we cannot reproduce his answers in full. The effort has been made to be totally objective in summarizing his answers.

The first question was addressed to Dr. Wilson.

## The Bible as History

The question was, "Is the Bible just the reaction of superstitious men to several chance encounters with beings from other worlds?"

Dr. WILSON: "The answer is a most emphatic 'No,' speaking purely from an academic point of view. Archaeology is my second hat (or my first — whichever you like), and archaeological evidence shows that the Bible is the most remarkably accurate history textbook the world has ever seen. Thus the answer to the question is "Most emphatically not."

The Bible touches all sorts of areas. It is an actual history of a people. The people are the Jewish people of course, and, if you like, it is written from their perspective. Who would have known, when the Bible records were written, that there would be all sorts of ways to check those records against other records of the past?

To mention just one area we have touched on to-night, we have glanced at the Assyrian period. As far as recorded Bible contacts are concerned, that period starts from the ninth century B.C. A whole series of Assyrian kings are named in the Bible, and there are a whole series of corresponding Bible kings — kings of Israel and kings of Judah, who are named also on the Assyrian records. We are just taking one example, in one period. As you study the records of the Bible in this Assyrian period, and then go to the Assyrian records, there are many records which show the same people in both records, each of course from their own perspective.

This is nothing whatever to do with superstitious men in contact with beings from outer space. The fact of the matter is that the more archaeology touches the records of the Bible, the more we find that it is a Book of integrity. It has been challenged in all sorts of places where it could not have been expected, and the more it is challenged the more it stands up to investigation.

Unfortunately my three minutes is up!

Mr. von Daniken declined to respond to Dr. Wilson's answer.

(The next question to Mr. von Daniken was garbled and the Chairman gave him another instead of it. It was later recognized as a question about the Piri Re'is map, and is included in Chapter 13.

•

### The Great Siberian Explosion

Question to Mr. von Daniken: "Do you believe that the great Siberian explosion of 1912 was caused by the crash of a space ship?"

VON DANIKEN: "I do not know. There has been a lot of speculation concerning this explosion in 1908." Mr. von Daniken referred to a book concerning that explosion. He stated that we still do not know what the real reason for the explosion was. "Everything is possible."

•

### The Bible and Other Religious Writings

Next question to Dr. Wilson: "Do you believe that the Bible is more accurate in information than other religious scriptures such as the Koran and the Vidas, etc., and how far do you believe in the Bible?"

WILSON: "The answer is, I do believe it is more accurate in its information than the books you have referred to. I lived in India for two years, and I know something of other so-called scriptures. The Bible is very much superior to any other religious text that I know.

How far do I believe in the Bible? Well, I believe in the Bible as a Christian. I am a committed Christian. I also believe in the Bible as an academic. I have lectured in many universities, colleges, schools and other places, in a straight-out academic manner. I have lectured in all sorts of ways about the Bible and history. At times it has been made clear when I have gone to a particular group that I am going as an academic, and not necessarily as a Christian with a point of view. I don't think I've ever been to one of those places (and I've been to some quite unholy places I assure you!) that I would not have been invited to come back.

I believe in the Bible as being more than a history textbook — that is the question: to me the Bible is God's revelation of Himself in the Person of Jesus Christ. To me the Bible is the guide for conduct day by day.

Mr. von Daniken declined to respond, except to say that it was not so to him.

•

### About U.F.O's

Question to Mr. von Daniken: "If we were visited by astronauts, why have they not shown themselves to the current time of modern society?"

Mr. VON DANIKEN made the point that we do not know whether they have or have not shown themselves, and he referred to U.F.O. cases. He stated that he had not personally seen a U.F.O., and he did not know whether, if U.F.O's do exist, they would be extra-terrestrial visitors. He expressed the view that in his opinion there was no doubt that they were here in antiquity.

He challenged Dr. Wilson's view that there is not one true case to support his view that astronauts have visited us: the record of the Indians with their straw garments was a pure case of astronauts visiting earth.

He referred to the problems of the distances between the stars and the universe as a reason why astronauts had not shown up, and there are great problems associated with time and space travel. Although two and a half thousand years might pass for us, this would not be so with a crew on a rocket ship. "Theoretically it is entirely possible that the same guys who were here in Biblical times will return tomorrow," Mr. von Daniken suggested. He conjectured that for them perhaps only five years had passed, and that was the reason why they had not recently returned.

WILSON elected to respond, and stated: "I touch on this whole matter of U.F.O's in one of my tapes at the back of this hall (this being an elaboration of Wilson's book *U.F.O's And Their Mission Impossible*). The whole concept of U.F.O's to me is a para-physical one, but that does not alter the reality of the beings — the sort of things described in *Close Encounters Of The Third Kind*. That is a novel, of course, but it is not nonsensical.

Today U.F.O. researchers of the highest caliber are recognizing that there are areas here that must be taken seriously, and there are some surprising statements by men of the type of Dr. J. Allen Hynek and others, men such as the late Dr. Edward U. Condon who headed up the Condon Report. Some of their statements are very surprising in their implications. Some aspects of these things touch spiritual areas, and I think that is beyond the purpose of our debate tonight."

•

### Do Satan's Angels Occupy U.F.O's?

Question to Dr. Wilson: "Do you believe that Satan's angels occupy U.F.O's?"

WILSON: "I made the point a moment ago that a subject such as U.F.O's could lead into another debate. I think Mr. von Daniken and I could debate all sorts of topics, and it could be quite interesting. I believe this.

"As for the question that is here, what else can I do but answer? Go to reputable researchers such as John Keel, or to Lynn Catoe, and there are similar conclusions. Lynn Catoe researched 400 volumes for the United States Air Force in her investigation into U.F.O. sightings, and I am quoting from the top of my head here — but she comes out with a statement to the effect that the parallels with the occult are very strong, and that the similarity to the demonology of the Middle Ages is striking — or words to that effect.

"John Keel comes out with the same sort of thing. He put out a book called *Operation Trojan Horse*, and he refers to 'a great cosmic put-on,' and he talks about great deceptions that are taking place. People may laugh at the whole idea of U.F.O's, and of contacts and so on, but if you do not laugh at them, and if you study the subject, you will find a couple of things that hit you.

"First, there are MANY parallels with the occult and there are MANY messages — if you like to call them that. There are messages that are very much opposed to the Bible, and which are very much opposed to Christian concepts, and which are opposed to Jesus Christ. Why? If U.F.O's are real, why this interest in the Bible?

"As to the question, 'Do you believe that Satan's angels occupy U.F.O's?' I believe that they are a Satanic thing — and so, yes, I do. You see, I believe in the Bible, and I believe in the God of the Bible. To me it is no great problem to be able to believe in a Satanic being, and in Satanic messengers as well."

●

### "You are Not an Atheist . . . Therefore?"

Question to Erich von Daniken: "You said you definitely are not an atheist, and therefore what do you believe in? What is the source of your authority for what you believe in, and how do you know without a doubt that what you believe is true?"

. . . . . . . . . .

"He's there to preach gods. And the fact that they are false gods doesn't affect his appeal. He is a prophet, but today he is no longer crying in the wilderness." — Graham Massey, in "The Case of the Ancient Astronauts."

. . . . . . . . . .

In his reply Mr. VON DANIKEN suggested that we assume that the gods had been here, and that by deliberate mutation they made our forefathers intelligent. He said that a question could be put to Erich von Daniken, "How have THEY become intelligent?" Mr. von Daniken could ask if they in turn had been visited from another solar system, and so this game could be played back through thousands of solar systems, and through billions of years, and it would not change anything. Eventually you are at the starting point where you have to decide with which religion you say "Here is God."

Mr. von Daniken made the point that you cannot decide where it started, and that it is somewhat like a circle drawn on a piece of paper.  If someone was asked where the circle started, his logic would say that there must be a starting point, but he would not be able to determine that point.

Von Daniken stated that by pure logic ultimately you come to what is meant by God, and so in that sense he was not an atheist.  He affirmed that he is a deep believer in a concept of God, but his God is something incomprehensible, unexplainable, a God Who is almighty and timeless, but is definitely not the figure who runs around with smoke, fire and loud noise, or who walks in a garden, or who has children, and such things.

(Dr. Wilson elected to respond.)

### The Use of Anthropomorphic Language

WILSON: "There is of course a concept called anthropomorphic language.  This means that there is a description of God in symbols and terms that humans can understand.  Thus when we read of God walking in a garden, or the eyes of God running to and fro through the earth, that is exactly what it is — concepts are put in such a way that we humans can understand them.  Ultimately you cannot philosophize your way to God.

"Not that it matters, but a cognate in my Ph.D. is philosophy.  Ultimately you do not work your way to God by a philosophical reasoning leading to a 'therefore.' What I find in the Biblical position is this: you take a step of faith to accept this God of the Bible, for the Bible says, 'Him that cometh to God must believe that He is.'  Having taken that step of faith, you find that it works out, and as you look back, you see that the evidences were there all the time — but there was first a demand for that step of faith.  I find that there is another logic associated with it all as I look back.

"Just in my one area of archaeology, and there are many other relevant areas besides mine, I find that the evidence is convincing.  I find evidence that this Book is beyond all books, that it is history written against the background of the times.  Its prophecies (such as where Jesus Christ would be born, and the sort of death that He would die) are all genuine.  They are set against the background of the times that are claimed for them.

"This being the case, I find it not very hard to accept the Bible's own statements that 'holy men of God spoke as they were moved by God's Holy Spirit.' This leads me back to the fact that there is a God. As for going back and back and back, ultimately you DO come to the First Cause. To me it is entirely satisfying, looking back, to find that that God is the God of the Bible."

•

### Why do Cosmonauts have Bare Feet?

CHAIRMAN: "This next question is for Dr. Wilson. He did choose to respond to the last question, and that is his option, but that does not mean he will be getting less questions. 'Why do all of von Daniken's space people or cosmonauts have bare feet? What did the astronauts wear on their feet? His one cosmonaut with his bare foot on a pedal, with a straight-forward gaze, reminds me of a church organist I knew.' Dr. Wilson, please read this one."

Dr. WILSON: "It is interesting that they do have bare feet. We have already discussed this one as a matter of fact. Of course, I simply do not accept that view: that particular picture we have talked about is of a man who is known in history, from the seventh century A.D. Seriously, why is he taking serpents out there into space with him? Is he going to need some antidote against other snakes, or what? It is not an astronaut — it is an interesting picture, but it is explainable, and it is set in known time. It is set in the seventh century A.D."

(Mr. von Daniken declined to respond.)

•

### Why No Continuing Formal Communication?

Question to Mr. von Daniken: "If man's roots go back to space travellers, why have they failed to continue formal communication?"

Mr. VON DANIKEN suggested that we had that before, "or something in the same sense." He explained that he had already said in his lecture that it was his opinion that we are intelligent beings, and that by simple means of intelligence we will have no alternative but to make space travel ourselves sooner or later. The other space people know it, and therefore it is not necessary for them to come back and to control every little thing that we do — because they know anyhow.

We humans know for sure that our sons will grow up, and that eventually they will have their sexual problems, their love affairs, and so even without our controlling them, these things are known — and there is no alternative. It is the same for these others who created our intelligence "after their own image." There is no need for them to come back every five minutes, for they know that we will grow up, and that sooner or later we will meet them in space.

•

### Haloes or Helmets in Drawings

Question to Dr. Wilson: "How do you explain the haloes or helmets on the drawings Mr. von Daniken displayed?"

Dr. WILSON: "How do I explain the haloes. Well, you can see the halo around my head! All sorts of things are put on pictures, and indeed I would agree with Mr. von Daniken that some of the concepts found on ancient things, such as pictures looking like airplanes, are possibly people thinking of air travel. This concept is known way back, and people have long talked about flying.

"Haloes are just another art form. I could ask you just as intelligently, Why do some Egyptian horses show two heads and a total of eight feet? or, Why did the Assyrian great monsters (those lion figures) have five feet? It is an artistic perspective for particular purposes. It is nothing to do with space people."

(Mr. von Daniken elected to respond.)

Mr. VON DANIKEN referred to the cargo cult of New Guinea as a very modern strange religion that has actually taken place. During the Second World War American airmen were in the South Sea Islands, and a number of little islands were used as improvised airfields. Directly after the war those airmen left, and nobody visited the islanders, and then about 15 or 20 years later some white men came back to the island. They found that the natives had perfected the old airfield, as though it had been in use. They had constructed primitive wooden cases and were talking into those cases for some hours a day, as though they were praying. This was because they had in mind what their fathers had told them, that when these beings from heaven with their apparatus were talking in some cases, new apparatus was coming down.

At that time the visitors gave the inhabitants of the island some food, chewing gum, cigarettes, and so on. So a modern religion called cargo cult has happened in our day, out of a misunderstanding. It has happened in our day, in the twentieth century. Why then should some primitive people, some thousands of years ago, not have made haloes?

(However, there is an essential difference. The New Guinea natives used objects and materials LEFT by their American visitors. Where do we find comparable materials left by astronauts? We do not find them.)

●

## What About Stonehenge?

A question was asked Mr. VON DANIKEN on his views about Stonehenge. In the preamble to his answer Mr. von Daniken made the point that he had been there, and that except for about five per cent. of the places mentioned in his books, he had actually visited them. The five per cent. where he had not been were places where he could not go, such as Russia or Red China, or some such place.

Mr. von Daniken referred to the argument that Stonehenge was a unique astronomical observatory, but that only the future would tell if that was the real and final answer.

Dr. WILSON made the point that he tended to agree with von Daniken, but that this was not the point von Daniken has made in one of his books.

VON DANIKEN: "In my books I never wrote about Stonehenge."

(We return to this after two other questions.)

●

## Ezekiel's Vision

The next question was to Dr. Wilson: "What is the explanation of Ezekiel's observation of the chariot?"

Dr. WILSON: "The explanation for Ezekiel's observation? Ezekiel says it was a vision. He actually says,

'I saw visions of God,' and as I read that particular chapter it shows something of the transcendence of God. He is the great God, the God Who cannot be limited in time and space.  In that chapter I do not see four helicopters moving in the same direction at once, nor do I see the type of concept associated with it being just helicopter-type vehicles.  Helicopters are limited as to their movements.

"The answer to the question is simple: Ezekiel himself said that he saw visions of God. They WERE visions, and in this we have descriptions telling us something about God."

Mr. VON DANIKEN: "It says that the wheels were full of eyes, roundabouts, etc. What a funny God."

Dr. WILSON: "It pictures the powers of God — the transcendence of God."

•

### "If You are Not an Atheist . . ."

Questions to Mr. von Daniken: "If you are not an atheist, are you a monotheist, or a polytheist?  How do you describe the god or gods you believe exist — are they personal or impersonal beings?"

Mr. VON DANIKEN stated that he had already answered a similar question, and had already made it clear what his concept of God was.  He stated that he certainly is not an atheist, and that he was not a monotheist, but that he is a deep believer in the concept of God "which I cannot explain, and which I try not to explain."  Mr. von Daniken stated that God is something that we cannot explain in words.  He pointed out that all his books in the United States have the titles of "Gods" — *Chariots Of The Gods?*, *Gods From Outer Space*, *In Search Of Ancient Gods*, etc.

He wished to make it clear that these titles were given by his American publishers.  He writes in German, and in the German versions none of his books had the title of "God" originally.  He claimed that the whole concept of God as it was described in his book was simply a misunderstanding, in his opinion, on the part of our primitive ancestors.  They saw beings coming down with noise, etc.

They were very respectful beings, with such things as weapons and lightning, and these beings had received the names of "gods." However, Mr. von Daniken claimed this was a misunderstanding. These gods had nothing to do with the real omnipotent God whom he himself meant.

•

## Stonehenge Again

The Chairman gave Dr. Wilson the right to respond.

Dr. WILSON: "I should like to respond, but I should also like to make a comment about Stonehenge."

CHAIRMAN: "Yes, go ahead."

Dr. WILSON: "Mr. von Daniken, in *Chariots Of The Gods?* at page 94, you state, 'The Egyptians fetched their obelisk from Aswan and the architects of Stonehenge brought their stone blocks from southwest Wales' — and so on. You do refer to Stonehenge."

Mr. VON DANIKEN: "That is the only phrase in the whole book."

Dr. WILSON: "Oh! Erich, Erich!"

(The context suggests that our ancestors "liked making things difficult for themselves and always built their statues in the most impossible places." He says, "I refuse to think that the artists of our great past were as stupid as that" and in the next paragraph talks about "the unknown space travellers . . ." (p. 94).)

Dr. WILSON: "As to the question about God.

"Mr. von Daniken is asked if he is a monotheist, and what is the concept of his God — a great God. I want to say very emphatically that the Bible concept is of God in plurality. "The Gods — He created," and there is consistency in Old and New Testaments as to the Person, the nature, the character, and the working of God.

"Here Erich von Daniken and I would be poles apart. I accept the Christian God, and I accept the fact that Jesus Christ is the Son of God Who came to give eternal life through His dying on a cross and rising again. Thank you."

CHAIRMAN: "Thank you, gentlemen. Ladies and gentlemen, the meeting is adjourned. Goodnight!"

•    •    •    •    •    •    •    •    •

The stated questions that follow were actually asked in writing, on the cards provided. They give the opportunity for a systematic answer to questions in the public mind, without the time limits of an evening's debate.

# Chapter 8:

# THE NAZCA LINES . . . BRASSY GOLD AND FOOTBALL FIELDS

At the end of the debate the Chairman of Campus Attractions (Mr. Jaryl Strong) made the point that many questions had been handed in, and he put on tape his statement that Mr. von Daniken had given Dr. Wilson permission to use the materials associated with the debate. Mr. Strong invited Dr. Wilson to comment on other questions. It should be remembered that some questions were addressed to Mr. von Daniken and some to Dr. Wilson. All the following answers are by Dr. Wilson. The opportunity has also been taken to summarize some of the major arguments against Erich von Daniken's hypotheses with relation to particular constructions and so-called mysteries.

•

### Nazca Lines

QUESTION: Why did the Peruvian Indians make the animal carvings in the desert floor?

They were animists, and probably they were making images of the gods associated with so-called animal deities, plants, and food.

•

QUESTION: If the drawings on the Plain of Nazca were drawn by the Indians as offerings to the gods, how were they planned if the completed drawing can only be intelligible from the air? (See points 9 and 19 below.)

•

QUESTION: Balloons do not need a landing strip and a vertical landing space, so vehicles should not need one either. True?

This is true. Also, some "mysteries" in other areas, involving (e.g.) a well-like hole, are supposedly caused by the space-ship's blast. The theory changes according to the local need! Even if an orthodox-type airplane were used, the terrain is quite unsuitable (see point 2 below).

QUESTION: Just how smooth are the so-called landing strips — could they facilitate a high-speed landing? (See point 2 below.)

•

QUESTION: Could the markings on the Plain of Nazca be marking lines of a city plan for a new city being built, perhaps by imperial decree? Could the same ruler have kept changing his mind after the original plan was marked in the soil, and kept changing his mind until the city was never built?

This would be very unlikely because of the close proximity of many of the lines, and also because many of them simply go around in circles or other patterns, running into each other and having no effective end. Others are clearly patterns of birds, monkeys, a spider, a whale, etc. They are not the plan for a new city.

### A Summary of the Facts

Clearly there is still a great interest in the lines on the Nazca Plain. The following summary will be of interest to many readers. Details can be found in Chapter 1 of *Crash Go The Chariots,* Chapter 6 of *The Space Gods Revealed,* and Chapter 6 of *The Past Is Human.*

Von Daniken says in *Chariots Of The Gods?* "The archaeologists say that they are Inca roads. A preposterous idea! What use were roads that run parallel to each other to the Incas? That intersect? That are laid out in a plain and come to a sudden end? . . . Seen from the air, the clear-cut impression that the 37-mile long plain of Nazca made on me was that of an airfield."

1.    Most of the Nazca lines are about four to six inches wide, and one inch deep. Some wider lines go for longer distances up to about 300 feet in length.

2.    The terrain is soft and sandy. According to Maria Reiche, a German scientist who has investigated the Nazca lines for about 30 years, any spacemen landing "would have gotten stuck."

3.    Reverend Donald Bond, a Baptist missionary at Nazca, has sent colored pictures showing that what are likened to "parking areas" for aircraft are only a few feet across. To think that these were parking bays is absurd.

Our artist has depicted the same "parking bays" to which von Daniken draws attention in *Chariots Of The Gods?* This area was presented in the television production, "The Case of the Ancient Astronauts," and it is only about 20 feet across, in total! It is part of the left leg of a huge bird (a condor) etched into the plain.

Von Daniken was challenged about this and he answered, "That's absolutely true. You are right here. This photograph which is in the original version of *Chariots Of The Gods?* is not my photograph, and even the legend on the right hand of the photograph was not

—Drawing by Lynette Hallihan
**Von Daniken's "parking bays" — a total of 20 feet across!**
**Von Daniken now says, "I fully admit . . . this explanation
. . . is simply ridiculous."**

made by me. It was too late to correct it. Anyhow, I fully admit that this explanation of being a parking place is simply ridiculous."

As the announcer for the film commented, "Ridiculous it may be, but after nine years it remains uncorrected in von Daniken's book. Many readers are being misled."

4. Von Daniken suggests that it is a preposterous suggestion on the part of archaeologists to suggest that these lines are Inca roads. He does not state which archaeologists have made such a suggestion. Von Daniken very often raises questions which tend to make his readers think there is a problem when in fact he himself is raising the problem. Archaeologists do not claim that the Nazca lines were ever roads. Properly made roads run through the Andes, and the roads gave cohesion to the Inca Empire. They are very different from the lines on the Nazca Plain.

5. Von Daniken elsewhere suggests that the NASA scientist Josef Blumrich was right in suggesting that Ezekiel's vision related to a space vehicle which could land vertically. Why then would space vehicles suddenly need these long "landing strips" at Nazca?

6. Did they have no braking systems? Do *airplanes* come from other planets? If they do they would need to choose better ground for landing!
come from other planets?

7. Some of the lines actually go up and down the foothills of the Andes — it must have been a very bumpy landing!

Sometimes the lines actually go over the edge of the cliff — surely a strange pattern for space-craft!

8. There is no evidence of a mechanical nature that the area was ever used as a landing field.

9. Maria Reiche has shown that geometrical principles were utilized in the construction of the huge figures carved in the desert, utilizing small models, rocks, and long cords. She elaborates this in *Time* magazine of 30th March, 1974. Miniatures about 6 feet square could have been used, and with long cords the drawings could then have been etched into the desert, using the model as a guide.

10. The people were animists, and they worshipped trees, plants, monkeys, birds, a whale and other objects

on the ground as well as things in the heavens above. This ties in with the concept that the etchings were associated with some of their gods.

11. It is also conceivable that the lines did involve some huge astronomical calendar concept, for computers have shown that the lines do point to various points associated with the stars, such as rising points at particular times of the year.    (This is elaborated at point number 16 below.)

12. Many of the fertility rites of the Incas were related to the planting of seeds and to the time of ploughing, and were very much tied in with the calendar.   The ancient Incas believed that heavenly bodies were very important in their daily lives.

## Tracing Movements of Stars

13. They had a great knowledge of the movement of heavenly bodies, and even had a tradition about tying down the sun, this being at the time of the southern solstice.   On that particular day, when the sun appeared to have reached its furthest southern point, certain ceremonial rites were performed.

14. The lines on the nearby cliff possibly represent a cactus plant, thus being associated with humanistic worship.   Others who live in the area believe that they depicted a candelabra (a lamp figure), thus pointing to more recent Roman Catholic worship.   Either interpretation would suggest that the lines had religious significance.

Many other drawings have been found high up the sides of mountains over the centuries, and they indicate that astronaut help was not needed.   One very good example is that of the descriptions on the Behistun Rock in ancient Persia, telling of the achievements of Darius the Great.   The buildings at Massada, 1500 feet above the Dead Sea, also illustrate man's ability without astronaut help.

15. Local people at Nazca say that many of the different lines follow the path of the sun over the year as it moves to the south and then to the north.

16. Astronomer William Hartmann, of the Planetary Science Institute in Tucson, Arizona, fed into a computer a question relating to the stars to which the lines pointed at any time between 5,000 B.C. and recent times.   The

print-out sheets were full, with stars at the end of each line.  This is not put forward as a conclusive argument, for it also implies that no matter where the lines pointed to, there would be stars in alignment, so vast are the galaxies in the heavens

17.  Von Daniken was not the first to suggest that the geometric design on the Nazca Plains looked like landing strips, possibly for inter-planetary aircraft.  The idea had already appeared in *The Morning Of The Magicians,* by the French authors Louis Paulles, Jacques Berigier, and Robert Charriux, published in 1960.  George Hunt Williamson's *Road In The Sky* also had a chapter entitled "Beacons of the Gods."

18.  These lines might well have represented constellations, or some sort of ceremonial pathways associated with priestly rituals, or a calendar with some astronomical significance, or something else.  Whatever the reason, it is clear that this hypothesis relating the lines to an ancient airfield is absurd.

## A Balloon Over Nazca

19.  Another way that the designs themselves could have been explained is that the ancient priests might have known how to move above the ground in a hot air balloon.  Ancient graves at Nazca have revealed that the people had finely woven textiles, and that these could have been used in the making of such balloons.  In November, 1975, a balloon was actually flown over Nazca and it had been constructed with only local materials. It was an 80,000 cubic feet, 7 storey high balloon named Conda I.  It carried as passengers Julian Nott, a British balloonist, and Jim Woodman of Miami, to an altitude of 600 feet (not for "a few seconds" as Mr. von Daniken has suggested).  The smoke and hot air were supplied from coals in a local clay pit, and the envelope of the balloon itself was constructed of the closely woven fabrics similar to those already known from Nazca.  The baskets, lines, and fastenings of the balloon were made from local materials such as reeds and fibers.  This is another possible explanation of how these strange lines could have been supervized.

20.  We have referred to Reverend Donald Bond, a missionary who has lived in Peru for many years.  He commented, "Obviously these ancient people were cap-

able of great achievements. However, what von Daniken says about the Nazca lines cannot be taken seriously. This makes me doubt his other conclusions also. I agree with you that his Chariots still crash."

•

## A Launching Pad on a Mountain?

QUESTION: Dr. Wilson, how do you explain the grooves cut into the mountains as shown in Mr. von Daniken's slide? Not the runway, mind you, the grooves cut in the side of the mountain.

The same picture is in *According To The Evidence* at page 321. The questioner says, "Not the runways, mind you" — an apparent reference to what were supposed to be runways at Nazca, to which Mr. von Daniken also referred. They were basically horizontal, across the Nazca Plain. How can we now have a launching pad running at an angle up the side of a mountain in Bolivia?

He surely cannot be serious. We have watched on television as NASA has launched rockets, and they go straight up. These channels are no more launching ramps than the Nazca lines are runways. The picture even shows that both channels are sealed at the top end of the so-called mountain — why would that be, if some vehicle was to go plummeting along them into the sky?

Von Daniken displays another picture with this one, and he shows water storage holes at its lower end. Somewhat similar holes can be seen at the base of his supposed launching pad. Were these channels also linked with water storage? I don't know, and apparently Mr. von Daniken does not know either, judging by his statement about them at the debate.

•

## "Why No Proof of their Presence?"

QUESTION: If these astronauts did influence our destiny, why did they not leave us mathematical proof of their presence?

In *Chariots Of The Gods?* Mr. von Daniken does suggest that written evidences have been left in various myths and legends. Wilson rejects that hypothesis, and does in fact accept the point of the question, that there are not mathematical proofs of the visits of these so-called astronauts.

Mr. von Daniken openly acknowledges that he has looked in vain for such an evidence that would be totally convincing.   He has hoped to find some records that would finally unlock the secrets of creation, and endorse his own hypotheses.

•

### "The Gold of the Gods"

The charges of "fake" made against him in various journals in relation to his book *The Gold Of The Gods* touch this matter.   There von Daniken claimed he had found the long-sought-for records of creation.   However, they were written on gold plates that were bronze after all, coming from a Roman Catholic church in Ecuador. They were supposedly found by Erich von Daniken in a technologically-impossible hall in a non-existent cavern.

This has been elaborated by Ronald Story.

In regard to that supposedly gigantic hall in Ecuador that von Daniken claimed he had entered, he actually gave measurements of 153 x 164 yards.   Von Daniken acknowledged in a debate with Ronald Story over TV in a program over WKBD TV Channel 50 in Southfield, Michigan (with associate host Jack Macarthy) that the "hall" had a smooth ceiling with no supports.

Ronald Story stated: "A friend of mine (Daniel Harris) in Tucson, Arizona, who is a Ph.D. candidate in astronomy, has calculated that it is actually physically impossible for a cavern that size to possibly exist, especially in an earthquake zone (which this is); but even not in an earthquake zone, because of the sheer stress of something like three million tons of rock (about ten tons per square foot) coming down on the ceiling of that cave.   And it is a common mining practice, today, to have supports about every 30 feet, to keep the ceiling from caving in.   So, in other words, such a thing as an artificial cavern, that size, with a flat, smooth ceiling, couldn't exist, physically."

After heated interjections from Erich von Daniken, the artefacts supposedly discovered in the cave were also discussed, and Ronald Story made the point that Pino Turolla, who was backed up by the Director of the Ecuadorian Museum, had shown that the artefacts pictured in *Gold Of The Gods* were actually obtained or photographed in the church of the Roman Catholic priest Crespi. Story stated: "Well, Turolla says, actually, they are not genuine artefacts at all. He says, as a matter of fact, they are contemporary trinkets, made by Indians that live there today."

### "It did not Happen," von Daniken Admits

In the film "The Case of the Ancient Astronauts," von Daniken says that the cave photographed in his book was not where he had seen the amazing things he writes about. The guide Moricz has emphatically denied von Daniken was in the cave he claimed to have entered. Von Daniken is asked in the film, "When you described standing dumbfounded as he switched on his light in the big hall, did that actually happen?"

Von Daniken replied, "No, it did not happen." He went on to claim the right to use facts so that the reader would be stimulated.

So when are we to know that von Daniken is using something as fact, or merely as dramatic effects? By his own admission he cannot be taken seriously.

It is all the more amazing, when we consider the facts, to read the opening lines of von Daniken's *The Gold Of The Gods*. "To me this is the most incredible, fantastic story of the century. It could easily have come straight from the realms of science fiction if I had not seen and photographed the incredible truth in person. What I saw was not the product of dreams or imagination, it was real and tangible. A gigantic system of tunnels, thousands of miles in length and built by unknown constructors at some unknown date, lies hidden deep below the South American Continent . . ." (p. 1).

Von Daniken will need to come up with some better "evidence" than this if he is to convince us as to the acceptability of his hypothesis! He continues to search for that elusive (because non-existent) proof. He seriously prejudices his credibility by giving arguments from these tunnels that he later acknowledges he did not enter.

### That Gold of the Gods in Ecuador: a Summary

1. Von Daniken has a whole book entitled *The Gold Of The Gods*, and one of the major topics is concerning a supposed vast network of underground tunnels in

Ecuador.  This is the basis for his title.  He claims that he visited the underground vaults with their discoverer, Juan Moricz.  In *Gold Of The Gods* he writes about a library that was full of metal plates, and tells us that many of these were gold, with strange writings inscribed across their face.  Those tablets told all sorts of secrets, including the amazing facts of creation.  Thousands of sheets of metals were inscribed, with evenly imprinted writing as though by a machine.

2.    So we find that Erich von Daniken is the great revealer of the secrets of the gods, and now he is able to give the answers to mysteries which have intrigued the world for long centuries.

3.    Even if it be argued that he did not actually see those sheets of metals (for he was never inside the tunnels), that is beside the point, for it is the spiritual reality of what he is describing that counts (?!).  We are supposed to have blind faith and believe what Erich has said, without any questions or reservations.

4.    Those non-existent plates are to give the answers to problems that scholars on earth today simply cannot resolve.  With his non-information from the non-existent tunnels and the non-existent gold plates, von Daniken will be able to tell of the new order that can be ushered in by accepting his strange new gospel.

(We discuss this somewhat elaborately in Chapter 1 of *The Chariots Still Crash,* and a great deal of further information is in the August, 1973, issue of *Encounter* magazine, published in London, England.  A further reference for this material is in *Der Spiegel* No. 12/1973 of 19th March, 1973.)

5.    It surely must be sobering to von Daniken fans to realize that his fantastic zoo, with its solid metal animal statues, its seven chairs of a strange material resembling plastic, and its library of two or three thousand metal plaques, were all in a tunnel which, on his own admission, he had never entered.

6.    There is in fact no such tunnel.  He claims that he had seen and photographed the incredible truth in person, and yet he later admits that he was never even in the part of Ecuador he mentions. (Page 9 of the *Encounter* article in an interview with two *Spiegel* editors.)

7.    Juan Moricz says that von Daniken had been shown a cave entrance in the Cuenca area, but the cave itself

was blocked. In any case, this was a great distance from the area that von Daniken claims in *Gold Of The Gods* to have entered with Moricz, complete with ropes, lanterns and all the rest.

## The Guide Admits . . .

8. Moricz himself admitted that he personally had never been into the caves, and that his claims were based on mythology. He acknowledged that many of the caves were actually formed by water erosion, but he believed that others were constructed by man.

9. Moricz is reported to have claimed that von Daniken had lied about the library and the golden zoo, and had "fudged" with his photos.

10. Many of the objects in Ecuador to which von Daniken refers are actually still in the church of the Roman Catholic priest Crespi, and the old man himself has difficulty distinguishing silver from tin, or brass from gold.

11. The archaeologist Pino Tirolla of Miami, Florida, has accused von Daniken of writing a fraudulent book with phoney pictures. Tirolla has given photographic evidence to show that the materials von Daniken is talking about are actually made in a little factory by local Ecuadorian Indians. They trade their junk to Crespi for clothes and small sums of money. (*The Space Gods Revealed*, p. 82.)

12. The Ecuadorian Government has checked out the cave story. They had already investigated the general area and found that no gold was in the caves they checked — only tayo birds (John Keasler , *Von Daniken's Golden Gods — Great Find Or Great Fraud*, *Miami News*, 17th October, 1973).

●
### Football Fields as Launch Pads?

QUESTION: Mr. von Daniken, assume that our civilization was annihilated by perhaps a neutron bomb, man-made ski jumps, and the like. Under your line of thinking what would these artefacts be? Air-strips? Launch pads? Runways?

I cannot answer for Mr. von Daniken, but over and over again I do get the impression that if there is a mystery, then that mystery can be resolved only by explaining that astronauts have visited us! Once again we refer to that rule in philosophy — the principle of

Occam's Razor, which should be applied.  If there is more than one explanation possible for one set of facts, the simplest explanation is the one we ought to adopt.

However, Erich von Daniken keeps on adding "ifs" and "Let us assume," and "Let us play a little game together" — then he jumps to successive conclusions from unproved hypotheses.  He takes all these random possibilities and decides that they add up to the certainty that astronauts have visited us.  He has virtually made a religion out of this concept of visits from spacemen, and we humans are so created as to need a religion.  Man has not found satisfaction, with science being put forward so often as a replacement for religion, and thousands have strangely and illogically flocked to the altar of Erich von Daniken.

Very possibly he would indeed expect the visitors to interpret the football fields and the ski jumps as airstrips and launch pads, as the question suggests.

At page 128 of *Some Trust In Chariots* there is an interesting picture that is actually supposed to be Santa Claus, and it is taken from the wall of an Australian kindergarten.  Then we have these satirical points, "What are the curious lines on the body?  What are the projections from the head?  Notice, too, how large and dominating the figure is made to be."

The point in that book is well made.  If one has a preconceived idea, it is possible to read that notion into all sorts of "evidences."  The Nazca lines can become a city plan, as one question suggested, or an airfield for space craft that apparently landed like aeroplanes.  Or maybe they were the football fields of this question!

.   .   .   .   .   .   .   .   .

"Von Daniken's thesis rests on inaccuracies, on distortions of the truth, on unrelated facts, and false similarities.  It denies man's ingenuity and abilities, and it uses phoney evidence in an attempt to prove its case.  Von Daniken's theories may be intriguing, and even attractive, but there's not a single solid piece of evidence behind them.  The achievements of the past tell us nothing about space men, but a great deal about the abilities and intelligence of our ancestors.  And if we ever are to find intelligent life among the stars, and that is a quest well worth pursuing, it will be because we continue to apply that inventiveness and that questioning spirit that the ancient astronaut theory seeks so strongly to deny." — Graham Massey, in the film "The Case of the Ancient Astronauts."

# Chapter 9:

# AN ARGUMENT OF STRAW

Von Daniken's argument about the straw figure is terribly weak, as we shall see. Nevertheless, on television in Australia (Wilson has a copy) he stated, in response to a question by his host, that this was his most pure case of a space-man having visited earth.

Two questions about the straw suits were handed in at North Dakota. In answering the first we show that von Daniken's basic logic is fallacious. Then we take the specific question and show FROM HIS OWN EVIDENCE that his hypothesis about the straw man is indeed an argument of straw.

## PART A: IT IS AN ARGUMENT OF FALLACY

QUESTION: Mr. von Daniken, why do the strange drawings have to be interpreted as space suits? It is entirely possible that they did not need space suits to survive here.

(The answer is by Dr. Wilson. See the next question and answer which deal more specifically with the particular case of the straw suits.)

The point in this question is well made. The problem is that Mr. von Daniken consistently regards cave drawings, etc., where there are helmets as pointing to astronauts coming with space suits. He has certainly pre-judged the issue, having decided that they must indeed have used space suits in our environment. However, some of his supposed astronauts on cave drawings are clearly naked. Mr. von Daniken certainly does confuse us!

Some drawings (such as of Darius the Great) are figures known in history — despite the "wings" drawn in association with Darius! This is another case where Occam's Razor should be applied, and NOT look for the least likely answer where simpler answers are possible.

As we said above, even if there is a resemblance to a space suit, that does not mean it WAS a space suit. I could ask, "Why, then, bare feet and bare hands? Why no eye-piece? Where is the breathing apparatus?" — for the head is completely covered.

Von Daniken's "Man in Straw" hypothesis is extremely weak. This becomes clear when we read the myth as it is given by von Daniken himself in "Gold of the Gods," including a magician cutting the cord binding the tribe to their home in the stars.

—Drawing by Lynette Hallihan

This "straw figure" is pictured by Mr. von Daniken at page 139 of his book *According To The Evidence*. He depicts a figure in a straw suit, and tells us that the Brazilian Kayapo Indians have made their straw suits in accordance with tradition. According to von Daniken, they are supposed to symbolize visitors from the cosmos. He tells us that these astronaut costumes are worn on ritual occasions.

### Now we use OUR Imagination!

In Australia, one of our early bushrangers was Ned Kelly, eventually hanged for murder. Ned Kelly had a protective helmet somewhat like that worn by these straw-suited figures that are depicted by von Daniken. What would my readers say if I therefore insisted that Ned Kelly had actually been in touch with these Brazilian Kayapo Indians?

This picture also reminds me of a welder, with his face protected against "flash" as he carries on his work.

Undoubtedly therefore the Brazilian Kayapo Indians must have been in touch with a colony of metal workers!

The picture also reminds me of goal-keepers in some ball games. Clearly therefore the Brazilian Kayapo Indians were world famous for their ball games — winners of many Olympic medals for sure.

If I insisted on any one of these explanations I would be accused of opposing Occam's Razor, and rightly so. Such a departure is true of Erich von Daniken.

My wife has just told me that the picture reminds her of somebody in an asbestos-type suit, able to go against a fire. Obviously therefore these Brazilian Kayapo Indians were the original fire-fighters, and had developed excellent suits for their work. We cannot of course understand why they were straw — but we do not let a little thing like that spoil a good theory. My wife WOULD be upset!

She has a good imagination, and she also says that the helmet looks like a waste paper basket turned upside down. I wouldn't have thought of that — woman's intuition, of course. No doubt these Brazilian Kayapo Indians were very house-proud, as my wife is, and this figure is simply of a man going out to collect litter, and he will put it inside the basket on top of his head.

Do not spoil this good hypothesis by suggesting that the litter will fall out once he puts the helmet back on his head. We do not want to be confused with facts, and as we do not actually know where the original figure came from, obviously we are entitled to speak authoritatively and declare that we know it is the litter man.

Did not the man himself tell us where he came from? He even described the very planet (as with some U.F.O. messages — with them, it is often the fictional Clarion). Once again, don't bother us with minor details that there is no such planet. The man said he came from a planet. We need no other proof, even though we don't know the planet. I know another man who came from there. Unfortunately he's locked up — I would love to have him meet up with his brother from space.

What I am saying, of course, is that even if the answer to a particular question is unknown, that does not mean that immediately we are forced to the conclusion that these must have been spacemen.

I am reminded of what the late Professor Fred Giles said at the end of an interview I had with him, as recorded in Chapter 9 of *Crash Go The Chariots*. Dr. Giles' final comments about von Daniken were: "He takes conjectures, accepts them as facts, builds way-out theories on them, and presents his 'many small coincidences' according to his own preconceived notions. He deliberately chooses the unconnected, weaves a semblance of connection around it, and presents his theories as foregone conclusions. This approach is often used by writers; it may make exciting reading, but one dare not accept it as substantially credible."

## A Parallel from Australian Cave Drawings

One other point is possibly highly relevant. One of our Australian authorities on aboriginal cave drawings is Ian M. Crawford, and he discusses at length the famous Wandjina Aboriginal paintings in the Kimberley Ranges, Australia, in *The Australian Aboriginal Heritage*. Von Daniken also refers to these paintings, including a picture opposite page 85 in *Gods From Outer Space*. At page 117 Ian Crawford comments concerning some of these paintings: "The illustrations of European sailing ships and sailors, which were incorporated into the myths, are examples of recent change in the art and mythology."

Despite Erich von Daniken's opinions of these Aboriginal cave and rock paintings, it is clear that many of them are recent, and if the older ones were not touched up constantly they would soon disappear. It is authoritatively stated (e.g. in *The Australian Aboriginal Heritage*) that they are touched up regularly, and this practice has been carried on for long periods of time.

The reference to Europeans, and to the visiting sailors and their ships, is highly relevant to this picture of the straw-suited men in their rituals. Around the world there have been various cultural incidents whereby it has been clearly shown that Europeans have been mistaken by the so-called native peoples for gods — partly because of their color; partly because of their vehicles, including aeroplanes; and partly because of their weapons, such as guns.

To see visits from astronauts from outer space as the only answer to myths and ritualistic ceremonies is simply not common sense, and certainly opposes the principle of Occam's Razor.

It is relevant to comment that in his books and at the debate he has referred to Aboriginal cave paintings.

## Those Australian Cave Drawings: More Awkward Facts!

Von Daniken makes various references to early Australian art. Thus at page 70 of *Gods From Outer Space* he depicts a ceremonial wood plaque from Central Australia, and then asks the question, "Is it a stylized prehistoric picture of the world or a drawing of a planetary system?"

The picture simply shows a series of circles moving out from a small space in the center, and these in turn are surrounded by 11 other circles. It would be just as sensible to suggest "Is this a tea-cosy surrounded by 11 cups?" or "Is this a round floor mat surrounded by 11 large coins?" It does not take much imagination to believe it is a picture of either. The trouble is that aborigines do not use tea-cosies, nor do they have mats in their "humpies" (huts). So of course let us again think of it being a picture of the world!

Von Daniken's style is to put forward a suggestion, and the implication consistently is that the explanation to the supposed mystery is that it is somehow associated with visitors from outer space. Over and over again the "mystery" is really of von Daniken's own making.

In the picture section of the same book, picture No. 33 is a rock painting from the central Kimberley district in Western Australia, and he tells us that it represents Vondjina, the mouthless mystical being of pre-history. (It is usually spelled Wandjina.) Von Daniken tells us that this is the personification of the Milky Way, and was an object of special reverence.

At page 26 of *Gold Of The Gods* he refers to cave paintings in these same Kimberley Ranges with the god's halo symbolizing the sun, and 62 circles being painted next to it. He suggests, "No one can seriously interpret the 62 small circles as 'suns'." (p. 27.) It is logical to ask, "Well, who *did* make such a suggestion?"

One of Von Daniken's regular methods is to put forward these hypothetical questions, and the fact that no one has ever asked them does not matter. His rhetorical questions are put in a very clever way, with subtle overtones that make out that somebody has put forward a suggestion, and that the "somebody" is really foolish to have done so. He uses that style at many points throughout his writings.

Being an Australian, I naturally felt it desirable that I should attempt to get material that would answer the absurdities put forward by von Daniken about these cave drawings. As a Senior Lecturer in Education at the Monash University, my own office is in the same building as the Center for Aboriginal Studies. In addition, I am a personal friend of Mr. Reg. Worthy, the Victorian Director for Aboriginal Affairs, a Federal Government Department. I also have contacted the Institute for Aboriginal Affairs in Canberra, and in these and other ways (including contact with missionaries to aborigines in Western Australia) I have come up with a lot of material relating to these caves.

Two fine books are *The Australian Aboriginal Heritage* and *The Past Is Human*. We shall refer especially to this latter, by Dr. Peter White, Senior Lecturer in Pre-History at the University of Sydney, Australia.

Dr. White discusses a number of the cave drawings. He is an expert in pre-history, and is an authority when it comes to Aboriginal culture. He tells us that "rock paintings from other parts of the world — Northern and Southern Africa, America, India, New Guinea and Australia — are all made in the entrances to caves, under rock overhangs or on boulders. They are exposed, even if only slightly, to rain, wind, dust, light, and temperature and humidity variations" (p. 26). He goes on to show that the paints used by the rock artists fade, crack and flake off, and that after several hundred years little is left of any of the paintings.

## Those Kimberley Drawings

He specifically discusses the Kimberley figures to which Erich von Daniken refers, in some detail. He points out that both males and females are depicted, and that their bodies are little different from any other paintings of humans except for the heads. He comments on the heads: "They are oval or rounded, and outlined with a red band like a halo. Sometimes the red band has a series of short, fine rays projecting from it, while in other cases a more elaborate structure of rays and semicircles is depicted. The only features are a pair of eyes and a vertical squared-off nose; neither mouth nor ears are indicated" (p. 72).

Dr. White describes the bodies in detail as to the patterns of lines and dots, and tells us that the Worora (the local Aboriginal tribe) believe that the Wandjinas were a previous population of semi-mythical semi-humans. The mythology is tied in with a previous great fight between the Wandjinas and Aborigines, and many people were killed. The mythical teaching is that other fights then developed between the Wandjinas themselves, and Wandjina individuals entered a cave or shelter, then transformed themselves into the paintings that we see today. Thus the Wandjinas actually become the pictures, rather than creating them.

### "Repaint them Frequently"

Dr. White then makes this highly relevant comment: "The Worora say further that their responsibility to these paintings is to keep them fresh and to repaint them

—Drawing by Lynette Hallihan

**Wandjina cave paintings, Kimberley Ranges, Australia. These are "touched up" regularly and are not "ancient" in the von Daniken sense.**

frequently, because if they fade and disappear so will the fertility of the countryside. They deny emphatically that they ever actually created the paintings or that they alter their characteristics" (p. 73). The Worora tribe inhabit the territory in which the Wandjinas are found.

Dr. White then actually discusses the conjecture that the Wandjina figures are accurate portraits of beings in space helmets, and he asks the highly relevant question as to how it can be explained that many of the figures have not only eyes but red eyelashes. "The red 'halo' — it is always red — looks very much the same as the band of red ochre the Worora men paint over the front part of the top of their heads and down the sides of their faces" (p. 73). He goes on to show that the men's hair sticks up behind the band, and that this looks like a series of small rays — it is nothing to do with a spaceman's antennae!

He goes on to tell the record of a Wandjina figure actually being painted by Aborigines in 1929.

Dr. White gives clear evidence that without continuous freshening up, repainting and care, these figures in the Kimberleys decay rapidly. He tells of photographs taken in 1901 which are compared with photographs taken recently, and they show that in that period of time considerable deterioration has taken place with some of the drawings. Dr. White tells us, "The extent of the damage varies directly with the degree to which the paintings are exposed to the weather, but we can estimate fairly generously that none of those now visible are likely to be older than several hundred years" (p. 74).

There are various other rock paintings in this area of Australia, and none of the figures are highly realistic. A kangaroo is recognizable by its stance and its leg proportions; dingoes (wild dogs) can be recognized by their head shapes, proportions and curly tails; and the drawings are not accurate or anatomically correct. There is enough given to identify them and no more. The same style is used in the drawing of these Wandjina figures — an outline and a body is given. It is simply a stylistic way of presenting the Wandjina. The "mystery" is actually of von Daniken's own making.

Dr. White makes a highly relevant comment: "Thus they are not portrayals of ancient visitors, but are painted according to a conventional Aboriginal style of depicting living creatures. To call them 'spacemen' is about as true as saying that Donald Duck is drawn as a shooter's guide to duck hunting" (p. 75).

Dr. White gives several reasons why these drawings would have been made. First, they are primitive art, rather like the children's art today. Secondly, they supposedly help a hunter, including a ritual spell. Thirdly, they are recording sacrifices made to clan spirits in crevices, boulders, and rocks, away from where the men themselves live. Sometimes they are possibly even a record of an historic event, and a reminder to the spirits to be grateful to these particular aborigines and his clansmen. At other times the drawings simply record dances, or unusual events such as twins being born.

It should also be remembered that various spirits believed that they themselves had a special relationship with particular animals who were drawn stylistically in their cave drawings. Ian Crawford (in his article *Wandjina Paintings* in *Australian Aboriginal Heritage*) tells of the myth of the ancestors of these people living on earth, having come out of the sky or the sea into the established land, and the belief that when they die their spirits actually remain in the paintings themselves. The Wandjinas are supposed to control the monsoon torrential rain, the lightning and the thunder, and so it was important that they be placated. Otherwise they would drown people in floods and kill them with bolts of lightning.

The Wandjina are consulted even as to who visitors are, and why they are coming. They are asked to cause fatal diseases to certain victims, or to give life forms to others. Ian Crawford also points out that "Wandjina caves were kept clean and tidy." He tells of some being maintained with fresh paint from time to time (p. 117).

He also tells us that the myths themselves change, for new episodes have been added from time to time. Even in this one generation some paintings have become so dilapidated as to become almost unrecognizable.

## PART B: IT IS AN ARGUMENT OF FANTASY

QUESTION: Dr. Wilson, how can you explain the straw suit which resembles a space suit worn by the natives?

Mr. von Daniken has referred to this as a pure case to indicate a visit by astronauts to earth. We need

go no further than one of his own books, *The Gold Of
The Gods*, to find that his most pure case is brass, just
like those so-called gold figures from the non-existent
golden zoo, in the non-existent huge cavern in an
imaginary subterranean passage in Ecuador.

To answer the question about the straw suits, let
us go to *The Gold Of The Gods*. His description comes
in Chapter 5, "On the Trail of the Indians." He tells of
a legend associated with the Kaiato tribe, given to Mr.
von Daniken in conversation with Felicitas Barreto, "a
Brazilian who is an Indian scholar of high standing"
(page 142). She had spent some 20 years living with
Indians in the forest. Von Daniken asked her:

"You know my books. What do the Indians have
to say about the idea that man comes from the universe?"
Felicitas Barreto answered by telling a legend relating
to the Kaiato tribe, and added, "Incidentally all the tribes
know this legend or similar ones."

## That Wicked Magician!

She then tells that the Indian Council sat on an
alien star and decided to change the tribe's dwelling
place. So the Indians started to dig a hole in the ground
deeper and deeper until it came out on the other side
of their planet. The chief was the first to rush into the
hole, and after a long cold night he actually came into
the earth. However, the resistance from the air was so
strong that he was blown back to his old home.

He told the tribal council what had happened, and
described the beautiful blue world he had seen, with its
water and green woods. The council decided to follow
the chief's advice to go to this world, and so he advised
them to plait a long cotton cord. Then they slowly
lowered themselves into the hole to avoid being blown
back from the earth. Because they entered the earth's
atmosphere slowly, their mass migration was quite successful, and since that time they have been able to live
on the earth.

They were able to maintain their contact with their
old home through the cord, but then a wicked magician
cut it in two, and ever since they have been waiting for
their brothers and sisters to come and find them again.
(Pages 143, 144.)

## "Countless Types of Masks"

Mrs. Barreto went on to say that the Indians talked to the stars, and that there are various rites associated with their star connections. Feathered men cover themselves with feathers from head to foot so that they will look like birds who can rise into the cosmos. "And then there are the countless types of masks, which, if one likes, can all be interpreted along the lines of your theories. Many of the masks have branches with several forks springing from them, like the antennae in your cave drawings. Often the Indians completely disguise themselves in straw to make themselves resemble their fabulous ancestors." (Pages 144, 145.)

Mrs. Barreto went on to describe the Kayapo Indians whom von Daniken has now taken as his pure case, to illustrate that there has been contact with the stars before Russian astronaut Gagarin had his first space flight in 1952.

Von Daniken makes much of the fact that Dr. Joao Americo Peret had taken photographs of the Kayapo Indians in 1952 and he tells us, "In view of this really astonishing masquerade I feel it is important to re-emphasize that Peret took these photographs in 1952, at a time when the clothing and equipment of astronauts was still not familiar to all us Europeans, let alone these wild Indians!" (p. 146).

## The Straw Man is Part of a Legend

To which we say, So what? Really, this whole thing is so ridiculous that it is amazing that people take von Daniken's writings seriously. Here is a man dressed in a straw suit. Obviously the people have had contact with white people, as Mrs. Baretto's own experience made clear — von Daniken himself referred to her as "a white woman." There are various legends of white people being accepted as gods by jungle dwellers, and there are all sorts of possibilities as to where they would have seen a suit similar to these straw suits — and the other "countless types of mask" to which Mrs. Barreto refers.

However, let us go on. The legend which is behind the whole matter of the straw suits is quoted by von Daniken in pages 146-150 of the above book. So that it can be seen that we are being objective, we shall quote several points from this legend, as he himself

gives it. The legend tells where the people lived, and
the mountain range could be seen nearby, its summit
being enveloped "in a cloud of uncertainty."

"The sun, tired from its long daily walk, lay down
on the green grass behind the brushwood and Mem Baba,
the inventor of all things, covered the heaven with his
cloak full of hanging stars." (*Gold Of The Gods*, p. 146.)

We then read of what happens if stars fall from
the skies. "When a star falls down, Memi Keniti traverses
heaven and takes it back to the right place. That is the
task of Memi Keniti, the eternal guardian." Now we
read of the arrival of von Daniken's visitor from the
stars:

"One day, Bep Kororoti, who came from the Pukato
Ti mountains, arrived in the village for the first time.
He was clad in a *bo* (i.e. the straw suit in the pictures),
which covered him from head to foot. He carried a *kop*,
a thunder weapon, in his hand."

## A European-type Weapon

We wonder of course if the thunder weapon was
in fact a rifle or some other European-type weapon.
Perhaps that's rather too ordinary, however! We go
on in the legend and we find that everybody was terrified,
and they fled into the bush. The men of the tribe did
their best to protect the women and children, and some
even tried to fight the intruder. However, their weapons
were too weak, and every time they touched Ben Kororoti
those weapons crumbled into dust.

No doubt this warrior from the cosmos laughed at
the weakness of those who opposed him, we are told.
To show them how strong he was he raised his kop and
pointed it at a tree, and then at a stone, and he was
able to destroy them both. (We wonder if it was not some
sort of a bullet that he fired!) The local people took this
as an indication that he did not want to be at war with
them.

The brave warriors tried to organize resistance
against the intruder, but in the end they succumbed to
his presence, for he did not harm them. Then we read
(page 147) about his appearance:

"His beauty, the radiant whiteness of his skin, his
obvious affection and love gradually enchanted every-
one."

That "whiteness of his skin" might be a give-away. Perhaps the visitor from space was just another European after all!

As we go on we find that he was not so affectionate or full of love after all, for before very long he is destroying his former friends right and left. However, before that happened he took pleasure in learning how to use their weapons. He became a good hunter, handling the tribe's weapons better than the best men of the tribe, and he himself was braver than any of them.

He was received into the tribe and was given a young maiden as his bride. Soon they had sons and a daughter whom they called Nio Pouti. One wonders of course how this visitor from the stars could blithely take a woman of earth and have children by her, but such problems do not seem to even occur to Erich von Daniken.

Next we read of Bep Kororoti instructing others in matters that they had not known before. He helped them construct a men's house, where the men would gather to tell their adventures and be instructed how to behave in times of danger. We are told that in fact the house was a school, with Bep Kororoti the teacher. It is of course entirely possible that there was some white man who had come to this tribe, and had brought them all sorts of knowledge from the so-called outside world.

According to the legend, various handicrafts were developed, weapons were improved, and all-in-all the tribe owed a great debt to this man with his tremendous knowledge. If necessary he would take his bow and make the young men submit to him. He was able to take his *kop* and kill animals also, without damaging them. To be horribly realistic, that is exactly what native people would think if a bullet was fired into an animal.

## The "Space Man" Aged!

We are surprised to learn (!), or von Daniken should be surprised to learn, that the man's behaviour changed with the years, for he appeared to age. We read at page 148: "He no longer went out with the others. He wanted to stay in his hut."

Then one day he "followed the will of his spirit," for he could no longer master it. Apparently the "space gods" had certain compulsions which were beyond their own power to control! He took his family with him, but his daughter Nio Pouti was left behind. He disappeared, but then he suddenly re-appeared in a village and uttered a terrifying war cry. The villagers thought he had gone mad, and did their best to calm him. However, when men approached him a terrible battle took place. Now we find that Bep Kororoti was not such a man of love after all, but instead, "his body trembled and anyone who touched him fell to the ground dead. The warriors died in swarms."

However, the story does not end there, for though the battle lasted for several days and there were swarms of warriors dead, we read that the fallen warriors could stand up again and continue to try to subdue Bep Kororoti. They followed him to the crest of the mountains and Bep Kororoti walked backwards, destroying everything near him with his *kop*. The mountain range, the trees and the bushes all turned to dust. Suddenly there was a tremendous crash that shook the whole region, and he vanished into the air surrounded by fiery cloud, smoke, and thunder.

Soon the bushes were torn from the ground, wild fruits were destroyed, the wild game disappeared, and as a result the tribe began to suffer from hunger. Then Bep Kororoti's daughter, Nio Pouti, told her husband she knew where there was good food, but that he must follow her to find it. He did so, and she looked for a special tree, then sat on its branches with her son in her lap. Now, we learn, at page 149:

"Then she told her husband to bend the branches of the tree down till their tips touched the ground. At the moment that this contact took place, there was a big explosion and Nio Pouti disappeared amid clouds, smoke, dust, thunder and lightning."

So Nio Pouti had also gone up in a spacecraft! — is that what Erich von Daniken is wanting us to believe? We read on in the legend, and find that Nio Pouti's husband waited for a few days. He was almost dying of hunger when at last he heard a crash, and then he saw the tree standing in its old place again. There was his wife, and Bep Kororoti was with her, and they had brought baskets full of food such as the people had never seen before.

Then the story goes on: "After a time the heavenly

man sat in the fantastic tree again and ordered him to bend the boughs down to the earth. There was an explosion and the tree disappeared into the air again."

Nio Pouti herself returned to the village, and under her instruction agriculture was systematically commenced in the village and the people lived in peace. We read (at page 150):

"The huts of our villages grew more numerous and they could be seen stretching from the mountains right up to the horizon . . ."

There is the legend. It is so full of typical mythical fairy-tale-type material that it is surprising that von Daniken would use it at all, let alone put it out as his pure example of a space man's visit. It is almost incredible that this is his chief evidence of such beings having influenced our civilization in days gone by!

## A Summary of this "Pure" Case

Summarizing, as this is von Daniken's "pure" case of a visitor from the stars, the following points are relevant:

1.    South American Indian tribes have legends involving the stars.
2.    They deal with such things as digging holes right through planets.
3.    Wicked magicians are involved in their tales about contacts with the stars.
4.    The tribespeople commune with the stars.
5.    "There are countless types of masks which can all be interpreted along the lines of your theories." They can be interpreted along various other lines also if one so desired!
6.    There is mythological language used with reference to the heavenly bodies, such as the sun lying down on the green grass.
7.    There is similar mythology about a falling star being brought back to its right place.
8.    The visitor's thunder weapon is remarkably like a shotgun or rifle.
9.    The man himself is apparently a "space god" who looks very much like the so-called white human races.
10. It was necessary for him to learn to use human weapons — despite his being a "space-god" he did not already have that knowledge.

11. He was able to have normal sex relations with a woman of the tribe.

12. They were able to produce normal offspring, which itself indicates that they were already of the same basic stock and no "cross" was necessary.

13. As the years went by he appeared to get older, and wanted to stay in his hut.

14. There came a time when he could not master his own spirit.

15. There is mythological and magical language as those touching him fall to the ground dead.

16. There is further mythology as those dead warriors stand up and continue their battle.

17. There is mythology again as everything near him is destroyed.

18. Bep Kororoti, the visitor, disappeared with fiery cloud, smoke and thunder, and then his daughter Nio Pouti took her place on the branches of a tree and she too disappeared with cloud, smoke, dust, thunder and lightning. The lightning is added as an extra effect now!

19. Then the tree comes back to its old place and Nio Pouti has returned and her father is with her.

20. After a time he sits in that fantastic tree again. The boughs are bent to the earth, there is an explosion, and once again the tree disappears into the air.

21. As a result of his great wisdom, and the instructions now given by his daughter, the village is at peace and agriculture is started, and the huts of the village stretch from the mountains to the horizon.

22. Such legends are found in many of the so-called Third World countries today. This author (Wilson) once collected a whole series of them in Fiji. They were tremendously interesting, and were courteously listened to as the old men told them. However, they certainly were not really believed in by the new generation of Fijians of today. Nor do we take Mr. von Daniken seriously as to his "pure" case of an astronaut visit to the Kayapo Indians.

## A MAN OF STRAW

**The fact is, von Daniken's "pure" case is indeed a man of straw. How amazing that the man would specially highlight such a mythological tale — and that so many people would be taken in by it!**

**Chapter 10:**

# HEART TRANSPLANTS, AND A SHIP IN THE SKY

We have considered the straw figures and the ritual followed by the Kayapo Indians. While we are in that geographic region, let us move to two other points of interest from South American culture. We refer to the so-called Stone Library at Ica in Peru.

First we consider a question dealing with what von Daniken puts forward as a heart transplant in ancient times.

•

### A Heart of Stone — Sorry, a Heart ON Stone

Perhaps the most interesting point made by Mr. von Daniken was in relation to his supposed heart transplant.

QUESTION: In that picture of Indians looking at an open heart, how does he know it's a heart transplant? Couldn't it have been someone examining the heart? It reminds me of ancient pictures of hearts being thrown to the gods — in the Egyptian scene of weighing the heart against a feather.

In the Egyptian *Book of the Dead* there are scenes where a human heart is supposedly being weighed against the feather of truth, the symbol of truth and justice. If there was sin on the man's heart it would weigh more than the feather, and the man's heart would be fed to the waiting crocodile god.

That is mythology of course, but nevertheless there WERE cases of human hearts being cut out and offered to the gods.

Let us relate all this to the supposed heart transplant pictured by Mr. von Daniken.

Three things should be said:

(1) Even if a heart transplant was attempted, what has this to do with visits by space gods?  Do we attribute every remarkable activity to such "outside" help?  Man has achieved amazing results in many areas, but there is no reason to keep on suggesting that astronauts came down and gave help every time there was (e.g.) a technological, scientific or medical break-through.

(2) It is possible, though not probable, that Peruvian Indians could have ATTEMPTED a heart transplant.   In his fascinating book *Noah's Three Sons*, Arthur C. Custance has written:

"Writing of Peruvian surgery, J. Alden Mason, quoting the well-known paleopathologist R. L. Moodie, has said (in Mason, J. Alden, *The Ancient Civilizations of Peru*, Penguin, Harmondsworth, 1957, pp. 222, 223):

"I believe it to be correct to state that no primitive or ancient race of people anywhere in the world had developed such a field of surgical knowledge as had the pre-Columbian Peruvians.  Their surgical attempts are truly amazing and include amputations, excisions, trephining, bandaging, bone transplants (?), cauterizing, and other less evident procedures.

"He then speaks of the use of anaesthetics and possibly hypnotics.  He remarks that some skulls show the result of operations on the frontal sinus.  Their 'operating rooms' were first cleared and purified by the sprinkling and burning of maize cornflour, first black, and finally white."

That is an exact quote, including (?) after the words "bone transplants."  If a ruler required a new heart, a strong slave might well have been the unwilling victim. Dr. Custance also reminds us (page 176) that the use of anaesthetic goes back to the Peruvian Indians with their coca leaves (whence our cocaine).  As we said above, such an attempted operation is not impossible. Its success would have been another story.

It is also relevant to point out that some of these Indians did offer human hearts to their gods.  This was especially so with the sun god — they believed he needed human hearts to give him the energy to continue his daily journey.  If the stones are genuine, they could be depicting that gruesome ritual.

## "The Pictures are Fakes"

(3) It is in fact clear that the pictures on stone are modern fakes. In *According To The Evidence* von Daniken tells of his own original doubts. Here are some of the things he himself has written about these stones in the possession of Dr. Janvier Cabrera:

"Professor Cabrera is a self-willed man. He does not easily tolerate opinions that run counter to his own, but he is as passionately interested in his collection as I am in my theory."

Is Professor Cabrera wrongly compared to Erich von Daniken? We expect and hope so. Von Daniken tells us how he came by his collection:

"Collector's pride. Cabrera has about 14,000 stones in his collection. The Indians brought most of them to his home and he found some of them himself."

Von Daniken tells us of his own nagging doubts about the genuineness of the pictures on stone. He tells us:

"I was constantly nagged by the question: are some of these stone engravings genuine (old) and some forged (modern)? And if there are forgeries, does Cabrera know about them? Is he a credulous, blind victim? Dr. Cabrera replied:

" 'In a village 26 km away there are forgers who copy the engravings and sell them to me, but I can tell straight away by the subjects which stones are genuine, I mean old, and which were forged and perhaps only made yesterday. In doubtful cases I have geological analyses made'."

### Fakes Sold to Gullible Tourists

Von Daniken sought out the man who made stone pictures to sell to gullible tourists, and he tells us part of the conversation:

" 'Do you also make large-scale engravings here?' I asked. The stonemason smiled proudly: 'Everything!'

" 'The big stones in Dr. Cabrera's collection have complicated historical patterns. Where do you get all your knowledge?'

" 'From illustrated papers.'

"Had I met genius?"

The "heart transplant" pictures were not similar,

at some points, to those that had appeared describing Professor Christian Barnard's work.

Von Daniken estimated that, quantity-wise, the pictures could have been produced by a forger and his "kindred," but Dr. Cabrera's method of testing under a microscope supposedly separated the fakes from the genuine stones.

However, we also noticed (above) that von Daniken himself said that Professor Cabrera "does not easily tolerate opinions that run counter to his own." Von Daniken also says he "is a leading surgeon" (page 322), and that he has obtained most of the stones from Indians. It is possible that they have "found" stones to "suit the tastes" of such a willing purchaser. This is at least a possibility.

### "The Ica Stones are Forgeries"

Von Daniken himself tells us, "When I saw the pictures I knew I would have to go there. But, ladies and gentlemen, don't think that I dashed off blindly! First I asked the archaeologist, Dr. Henning Bischof, of the Volkerkunde Museum in Mannheim, if he knew of the engraved stones from Ica and what he thought of them. Dr. Bischof wrote, saying that the Ica stones were forgeries which the Indians made to sell to tourists for a few soles (Peruvian coin). Unlike my opponents, I am always ready to hear both sides. Now I knew that official archaeology looked on the engraved stones from Peru as forgeries."

Von Daniken tells us further, "I admit that I was still gnawed by doubt when we met again in Cabrera's house. I told him so." He then became convinced by Professor Cabrera's argument that the genuine pictures were covered by oxidation, and when examined microscopically, the fakes were not so covered, supposedly indicating that the stones were engraved before the oxidation set in.

That, however, is by no means convincing. This author (Wilson) has been involved with archaeology long enough to know that faking of artefacts is a highly lucrative business. Debates on such issues have occurred occasionally in prestigious journals, with archaeologists of repute on both sides. The fakes are not always easily discerned.

As for carvings on stone, even a simple process such as immersing of the stone in hot water can drastically affect the surface. This would lead to a chemical reaction that could in turn involve a chemically detectable change in the outer film of the stone.

We have no reason to believe that known forgers who "put it over" tourists would be above using known "tricks of the trade" for bigger game than tourists! A "heart surgery stone" would be ideal for "a leading surgeon."

—Drawing by Lynette Hallihan
**One of von Daniken's "heart transplant" pictures.**

In the film "The Case of the Ancient Astronauts" . . . it is clearly stated that the local Peruvian artisan Brazilia claimed to have produced the "heart transplant" picture on stone for Dr. Cabrera, which Dr. Cabrera denied. However, Brazilia produced a statement signed by Dr. Cabrera thanking him for his co-operation in producing the stones. Brazilia re-produced another heart transplant picture on stone in about an hour, then treated it with donkey's dung and boot polish to give it an aged look. Brazilia acknowledged his work is NOT ancient. The Institute of Geological Sciences in London reported that a supposedly ancient Cabrera stone submitted to them for analysis was in fact recently worked. The physical make-up of the stone was the same as one submitted from Brazilia.

So the "heart transplant" pictures are modern, not ancient. Crash go the Chariots yet again!

## A Ship in the Sky

According to von Daniken (in *According To The Evidence*), the same stones also show Peruvian Indians worshipping a ship in the sky. I am reminded of a verse in the Bible, Habakkuk 1: 16, giving a parable about fishermen—

"Therefore they sacrifice unto their net,
and burn incense unto their drag . . ."

These Peruvian Indians knew about fish, according to von Daniken himself, and lived near the Pacific coast. It is entirely likely that they, too, would worship "the god of ships," just as many other peoples have done their best to placate the supposed gods of the crops, and rain, and so many more in ancient times.

What has this to do with a visit by astronauts? Did they see the "astronauts" in ships? We thought from von Daniken that they came from the skies, and landed on imaginary "runways" such as those at Nazca. Something's wrong somewhere. Maybe Mr. von Daniken's space-vehicle is on board the sailing ship! Someone should ask him about that. They should also ask if Brazilia created these "ancient" artefacts also.

**Chapter 11:**

# WORSHIPPING AN INVISIBLE
# DOG STAR

We move from the supposed worship of a ship in the sky to the actual worship of a virtually invisible star by the Dogon tribe in West Africa. The star is Sirius B, companion to the Dog Star, Sirius A. This is elaborated by Robert Temple in his book *The Sirius Mystery*, and has been taken up by Erich von Daniken, as was shown in the debate at North Dakota.

The existence of Sirius B has been confirmed only in the last century. Therefore how can we explain the traditional knowledge of its existence by a supposedly primitive tribe?

QUESTION 1: Dr. Wilson, could you explain why the evidence about Sirius does not support the proposition? Or where the natives received the knowledge?

QUESTION 2: Can you explain how the African tribe knew about Sirius A and B?

QUESTION 3: Dr. Wilson, how do you explain the precise configuration of Sirius, lacking modern tools of observation?

QUESTION 4: Tell us about the observation of the Super Nova of 1054.

Once again, there are several possible explanations for the Dogon tribe's knowledge of Sirius B. Applying Occam's Razor again, Mr. von Daniken's hypothesis will be rejected!

Knowledge of Sirius A (question 2) is no problem. Sirius A is the "Dog Star" and is readily visible.

The knowledge about the relationship of Sirius B to Sirius A is not precise (question 3), though the revolution figure of 50 days is approximately correct. "Fifty" was also the number of oars associated with the mythological ship "Argo" and in *The Sirius Mystery* (page 80) Robert Temple suggests a possible association of the "fifty" in each case.

There is also a major error in the tradition handed down by the Dogon.  Sirius B and the supposed Sirius C are said to come closest to each other every 32 years, but this cannot be worked out by computers unless the two stars travel in opposite directions, and the priests of the Dogon tribe insist that they travel in the same direction.

Various authorities suggest that the natives could have received the knowledge (question 1) from several sources:

The natives could have received the knowledge (question 1) from several sources:

(a) Anthropologists;
(b) Missionaries;
(c) University-trained persons, for University education is no longer "new" in Africa: cross-cultural communication could be the explanation;
(d) Guesswork — as suggested by the Science correspondent of the Australian Broadcasting Commission in an Elizabeth Bond talk-back program in April, 1978, at the time of a von Daniken visit to Australia;

### The Flare of a Super Nova?

(e) By actual observation associated with the flare of a super nova.  The one referred to (genuinely!) in question 4 was described in the Melbourne *Herald* of March 15 as follows:

"On July 4, 1054, Chinese astronomers saw a great star appear in the sky and marvelled.

"Gradually it began to disappear.

"The record in the chronicles of the Peking Observatory reads:

" 'In the first year of the period Chihha, the fifth moon, the day Chi-Chou, a great star appeared approximately several inches south-east of T'ien Kuan. After more than a year it gradually became invisible.'

"Today, if you look at the spot in the heavens you will see a great expanding cloud of gas called the Crab Nebula, which seems as if it were caused by some gigantic explosion.

"Astronomers believe the star the Chinese saw was a super nova, a massive star which collapsed and exploded.  The Crab Nebula is all that remains of it."

If that could happen with relation to the Crab Nebula it could well happen to Sirius B also.

(f)    Possibly, but not probably, by the use of a primitive telescope. In *Noah's Three Sons* Dr. Arthur Custance has this highly relevant quotation from Gilbert Lewis in "The Beginnings of Civilization in America" (American *Anthropologist*, New Series 49, Jan.-Mar., 1947, p. 8 and footnote). Lewis has written:

"Probably the most remarkable achievements of the American Indians were in the fields of arithmetic, astronomy and the calendar. Two of the greatest inventions of arithmetic, the zero and the sign of numerical position, were regularly employed in America long before they were known to have occurred elsewhere . . .

### "The Possible Use of Astronomical Instruments"

"It may be noted that a few apparently unrelated items which I have discovered in literature may, when put together, suggest the possible use of astronomical instruments in early America. Both in Mexico and Peru concave mirrors were found, articles that had not been seen in Europe at the time of the Conquest. In Peru, these concave mirrors were employed in a solar rite. Periodically all old fire was extinguished and a new fire was started by the priests who, with these mirrors, focussed the rays of the setting sun on a wisp of cotton. Among the Aztecs new fire was produced at night by the fire drill. However, that they had recollections of a practice akin to the Peruvian is suggested by the name of one of their chief gods, 'Smoking Mirror'."

(g)    In the debate at North Dakota I referred to Betty Hill having information about a star's location, received at the time she and her husband Barney were supposedly abducted by a U.F.O. Under hypnosis she gave previously unknown details of the star's location, and later she was shown to be correct.

The relevance is that if U.F.O. contacts are Satanically engineered (as argued in *U.F.O's And Their Mission Impossible*), the same sort of information could also have been given to the "witch doctors" of the Dogon tribe.

It should be remembered that the sun, the moon, and the stars have all been worshipped through the ages. It is false worship of course, and is part of the Satanic counterfeit to turn men away from the true God. Satan, called in the Bible "the prince of the power of the air," would have men worship the things of creation rather than the Creator Himself. Thus it would be entirely likely that demons pass on certain knowledge, especially if it could lead to challenges against the true God, and so be a means of confusing men and leading them to a belief about visitors from outer space.

That is what is happening with the present wild speculation about visitors coming from outer space in U.F.O's. The evidence is overwhelming that U.F.O's are a Satanic manifestation of power. Jesus warned that in a last generation there would be signs and wonders in the heavens, and that Satanic signs would even deceive, if possible, the very elect.

This may NOT be that last generation, but Satan and his demons would not know that. They would, however, know the teaching, and would recognize possible implications for themselves. This point of course is acceptable only to those who believe in demons, and that includes Bible-believing Christians and many others who have lived in "eastern" countries, as this author has done.

Robert Temple, the author of *The Sirius Mystery*, which von Daniken quotes concerning Sirius A and Sirius B, actually discusses the association of the Dog Star with the ancient god Anubis. It had a man's body and a dog's head. The ancient belief was that Anubis was the son of Nephthys, the sister of Isis, and the tradition was that Nephthys was invisible while Isis was visible. The companion of Isis was Osiris, equated with Ra the sun god — Ra was the god of the day and Osiris was the god of the night. Osiris is also at times identified with Anubis, the dog-god. (Page 80, *The Sirius Mystery*.)

Actually there is considerable interchange with the gods, both in one country and between countries — e.g. Baal of Canaan was Hadad of Syria. In Egypt, Ra was the sun god and he is at times equated with Osiris. Osiris "took over" from Ra at night-time, and so was the god of the underworld. As the sun disappeared, so Osiris also is invisible and is associated with the worship of an invisible dog star. As we have said above, Osiris is also specifically identified with Anubis.

There is also a connection with ancient Babylonians. Robert Temple points out that the famous Egyptologist

Wallis Budge was convinced that Egypt and Sumer each derived their culture from a common, exceedingly ancient source. (*Ibid.*, page 80.)

In early times of Sumer the chief god Anu was pictured as a jackal, which is again a variation of this dog motif.  Both Egypt and Sumer worshipped the dog god, with secret mystery rites that had Satanic overtones, with certain rituals restricted to initiates.

—Drawing by Debra Wilson

**Anubis, the Egyptian dog god, associated
with Sirius A, the Dog Star**

## "The Black Rite" in Ancient Times

The association of Sirius A and B, with religion is further elaborated by Robert Temple. He states:

"There is evidence that 'the Black Rite' did deal with astronomical matters. Hence the Black Rite concerned astronomical matters, the black Osiris and Isis. The evidence mounts that it may thus have concerned the existence of Sirius B.

"A prophecy in the treatise 'The Virgin of the World' maintains that only when men concern themselves with the heavenly bodies and 'chase after them into the height' can men hope to understand the subject-matter of the Black Rite. The understanding of astronomy of today's space age now qualifies us to comprehend the true subject of the Black Rite, if that subject is what we suspect it may be."

Robert Temple says in *The Sirius Mystery* that the knowledge of Sirius B comes from Egypt, and was known some 3,000 years ago. He suggests an earlier impartation of knowledge from Sirius B itself. However, Temple himself has omitted certain evidence that did not suit his interpretation, apparently considerng it to be irrelevant or important. The Dogon tribe describe the star's orbit as being like that of an egg's shape, with the stars inside and not on the path itself. They have a third star (Sirius C) which the most modern equipment cannot find, and there are many other symbols representing mythical beings.

It is stated in "The Case of the Ancient Astronauts" that "in Temple's book these last symbols are omitted, and the diagram turned around so that it more closely resembles the true astronomical position. So only the parts that fit the picture have been selected." That is understandable, though regrettable. Temple obviously believes the facts can be interpreted as he has done.

The knowledge given to the initiates could certainly have included certain specific facts about Sirius B. If we can accept the fact that demon worship was and is rife in Africa, it is more than a possible answer. It would be the probable answer — and its details can be derived (as shown above) from *The Sirius Mystery*, the very source quoted by Erich von Daniken.

## How Old are the Stars?

The above explanations are interesting and relevant, but there is another which is perhaps even more likely, though opposing present teaching of astronomy.

Temple's book is reviewed in *Nature*, Vol. 261 of June 17, 1976, by Astronomy Professor Michael Ovendon of the University of British Columbia, Vancouver, Canada. He points out that "in the 16th Century, at Timbuktu in Mali, there flourished a leading university of the Muslim world." He also acknowledges that there is mystery associated with Sirius B, as when he says that Sirius B's extra brightness when it is nearer to Sirius A is not "explicable by present ideas."

That statement set me thinking, and I read again a report by astronomer Stephen P. Maran, a researcher at NASA's Goddard Space Center in Greenbelt, Maryland. He talks about Sirius B in an article entitled *Red, White and Mysterious* in *Natural History*, Vol. 84, No. 7, August-September, 1975.

## The White Dog Star was Red in "Recent" Times

Maran also brings out some data that is not explicable by present ideas. He reminds us that in ancient times Sirius A (the Dog Star) "was referred to as red; (whereas) today it has a brilliant white color, but no physical theory yet proposed can account for the change" (page 82). He says that "Sirius B appears to be much older than Sirius itself, although, according to accepted theory, the two stars should have been born together."

The complexity of the problem is seen when we consider the argument that Sirius B might have been a red giant only 2,000 years ago (page 86), with the ancient red color coming from Sirius B and not Sirius A. Maran rejects this, and points out that "even optimistic astronomers calculate that the time required for a red giant to become a white dwarf is much closer to 100,000 years than to 2,000 years" (page 86). He quotes Malcolm P. Savedoff, a University of Rochester astrophysicist, as concluding that modern astrophysics cannot account for the alleged red color of Sirius in historical times.

Maran has much more to say — if they were formed together, why is Sirius B already a white dwarf and Sirius A not yet even a red giant? Did matter from Sirius B

contaminate Sirius A?  He tells us of the puzzles be-
setting stellar experts, and then comments:
        "If the experts are correct, then Sirius B was once
    a massive red giant that would have been bright
    enough to attract the attention of observers on earth"
    (page 87).
        Then Maran gives his own objection to this hypthesis
— "that if there were men around on earth to see this
postulated red star, they must have been Neanderthals
or members of some other, now extinct prehistoric race.
It seems inconceivable that such observers, if they noted
the phenomenon, could have passed the knowledge on
down to the time of the early Christian era."
        In the first century B.C. Horace referred to Sirius as
"the red dog star," and in the following century Seneca
said Sirius was redder than Mars (page 82).   About 140
A.D. Claudius Ptolemy listed Sirius as one of six reddish
stars.   In the 10th Century A.D. the Arab astronomer
Al-Sufi the Wise recorded it as white.   Was it Sirius B
(not A) that was observed 2,000 years ago?   This would
explain the red (not white) color.   As Maran says, "The
ancient red color of Sirius would have come, not from
Sirius A, but from Sirius B, which in those times would
have been larger, brighter and redder than it is now"
(page 86).   Maran acknowledges the problem that such
an explanation would oppose present theories as to the
life cycle of stars.

### An Interaction between Sirius A and Sirius B?

        Yet another possibility (mentioned above in passing)
is that there has been an interaction BETWEEN the two
stars, with some of the matter of Sirius A being lost to
Sirius B.   Stephen Maran talks about the calculations of
the Dutch astronomer E. P. J. van den Henvel, showing
that "in certain cases a close binary system can undergo
mass transfer, with the larger star losing up to almost
90 per cent. of its mass . . ."   Maran relates this to Sirius
A and Sirius B, with the possibility of material from the
then larger Sirius B having been transferred to Sirius A.
        Maran suggests that the unusual phenomena asso-
ciated with Sirius A could then be understood, though
another problem is raised.   How could such changes have
occurred in only 2,000 years, and not in prehistoric times?
However, dating is notoriously subject to change these
days, as anthropologists, archaeologists and geologists

are very aware.    It is possible that there will be re-thinking in these areas by reputable astronomers.    It seems it might be necessary, for certainly authorities have differing opinions on some of these matters.

Here are experts giving tentative answers, and acknowledging a series of paradoxes.    One other possibility should be considered, and that is that such changes have not taken the extremely long periods of time being postulated.    This is opposed to present opinion in astronomy circles, but it is not without some support.    This author (Wilson) heard Professor Harold Slusher, of Texas State University, at El Paso, lecture at Grand Rapids in November, 1976.    He argued brilliantly for much shorter periods of time being involved in stellar activity.

The Austrian astronomer, Karl Rakos, concluded in 1974 that Sirius B was "the brightest and hottest white dwarf we know" (page 82), and this "revived the suggestion that Sirius B might actually have been a red giant only 2,000 years ago" (pages 82 and 86).

If a red giant (Sirius B) COULD have become a white dwarf (again, Sirius B) in 2,000 years, this information might well have been known to selected persons through whom the information was handed down.

Such an explanation "contradicts much of what we know (or think we know) about the life cycles of stars" (page 86).    So what?    Obviously that "knowledge" is not as established as was thought even a decade ago.

Perhaps Professor Slusher is right: if he is, it is probable that Sirius B WAS observed by ordinary humans 2,000 years ago, and this could be the explanation of the knowledge handed down through the centuries to the priests of the Dogon tribe.

In any case, we have shown that logical answers are possible. The application of Occam's Razor will certainly again rule out von Daniken's astronaut hypothesis.

## A Summary

Because some of the above material comes from scholars with opposing views, it at times is contradictory.    To simplify the arguments, we include the following summary:—

1. The Dogons (and other African tribes) did worship the dog star in ancient times.    It was also worshipped in Egypt, across the other side of the continent, and in Babylonia.

2. There are apparent errors as well as truth in the Dogon traditions handed down through the centuries.

3. Those who reject the "ancient knowledge" tradition suggest the information about Sirius B was gained from anthropologists, missionaries, university-trained persons, guesswork, the observation of the flare of a super nova, or even by the use of a primitive telescope.

4. There was a secret Egyptian "black rite" involving both Sirius A and Sirius B. Such demon worship was rife in Egypt and the ancient world in general. Certain knowledge about the stars was given to initiates.

5. Sirius A was recorded as being red (not white) 2,000 years ago, an unexplained phenomenon by modern theories of astronomy. As a virtually invisible white dwarf, Sirius B "should" be older than Sirius A, but apparently it is not. According to most astronomers, theoretically the two stars should have been born together and should manifest similar qualities, but they do not.

6. Some authorities conjecture that it was Sirius B (not Sirius A) that was seen (as a red giant) 2,000 years ago: that would leave the problem of how a red giant could become a white dwarf in the brief time of 2,000 years.

7. There has possibly been interaction between Sirius A and Sirius B, with Sirius B losing much of its mass to Sirius A. Thus both stars might once have been visible to the naked eye.

8. Possibly the time involved in the life cycle of stars is not as great as has been traditionally believed.

9. The application of Occam's Razor should rule out "astronaut visits."

**Chapter 12:**

## U.F.O's . . . THE BERMUDA TRIANGLE . . . THE PYRAMIDS . . . "PYRAMID POWER" AND "PYRAMIDOLOGY"

### Where do U.F.O's Come From?

QUESTION: Where do the U.F.O's ALL come from?

In my book *U.F.O's And Their Mission Impossible* we elaborate the various theories as to where U.F.O's come from. We give documentary evidence to show that we must accept the fact of U.F.O's, and we illustrate from the credibility of the witnesses. These objects are witnessed by doctors and lawyers, pilots and navigators, men and women, and many other members of society. Contact has been made, and some of the tales of contact are virtually incredible.

The U.F.O's do not come from either U.S.A. or U.S.S.R., for each country earlier thought that the other had some unexplainable power beyond their own achievements. U.F.O. entities are friendly only to the extent of attempting to gain confidence: over and over again they have left very unfortunate results in their dealings with humans, including actual illness and death.

There have been hoaxes and hallucinations of course, and sometimes natural explanations have been put forward, including sightings of the planet Venus, unusual cloud formations, airplanes, etc. Other explanations have ranged through a hollow earth, a parallel world, or the possibility of a hidden planet.

All of these are shown to be unacceptable in *U.F.O's And Their Mission Impossible.* We then come down to two possibilities. The first is the possibility of some great nation utilizing electro-magnetic power and an anti-gravitational beam; second, coming from "space." We make the point that the Condon Report of 1969 rejected this view, and leaned towards the para-physical argument.

In *U.F.O's And Their Mission Impossible* we also come down to the para-physical explanation, and we discuss the fact that there are many parallels with happenings associated with the occult. Ultimately we come to the point, based on objective evidence, that U.F.O's are a Satanic device. They are basically evil, and they are a special phenomenon of the generation we now live in. This "demonic argument" is not limited to writers with a strong Christian commitment. Because of parallels with historic happenings associated with demonic forces, the argument has been acknowledged by researchers as demanding credence.

•

QUESTION: Mr. von Daniken, what happened to the story of astronauts landing because of a malfunction in their craft? They left a record of their crash.

There are many examples in the U.F.O. literature of U.F.O's landing and supposedly having trouble, and having to repair their craft. There has never been part of a U.F.O. recovered, nor have any of their tools been found. Wilson believes that U.F.O's are a very real phenomena, but that their explanation is in the paraphysical realm. We have already said that this leads to the demonic argument.

The question above is probably referring to the time when very little men were supposedly found associated with a crashed spacecraft. This has been checked out and authoritatively denied, but the story still keeps "popping up."

•

QUESTION: Mr. von Daniken, if so many visitors came to so many people so long ago in their primitive state to enlighten them, why haven't we in all our superiority been visited as a people worth being advanced further than what we are?

Dr. WILSON: In this debate Mr. von Daniken suggested the possibility that some U.F.O. visitations were visits of spacemen. He did not elaborate the theme of U.F.O. visits. He does have three visits now, the last being "in Bible times." Perhaps we are due for some more soon!

## The Bermuda Triangle

QUESTION: What is the connection (if any) between U.F.O's and the Bermuda Triangle?

In the revised version of *Crash Go The Chariots* I have a chapter dealing with the Bermuda Triangle. Most of the material there is selected from Lawrence David Kusche's excellent book *The Bermuda Triangle — Mystery Solved* (available from Warner Books, New York, at $1.95). Several points should be made:

Many of the incidents supposedly associated with the Bermuda Triangle are fictional.

Quite often the records have not been sufficiently checked.

When the records are checked there are often natural explanations for the disasters.

Sudden sinkings, etc., take place around the world: they are not necessarily "mysteries."

Many of the disappearances actually become "sinister" only in later reporting.

There is a great deal of misreporting and sensationalism associated with the Bermuda Triangle.

There are many incidents of disappearances in the Bermuda Triangle that are associated with bad weather and natural phenomena.

(In *Crash Go The Chariots* we give examples to substantiate these points of view.)

I personally do not see a great deal of connection between U.F.O's and the Bermuda Triangle, but it is of course possible that some U.F.O. activities and mysteries could well be associated with the Bermuda Triangle as with any other areas of the world's surface.

The U.F.O. phenomena is very real, and so could be associated with that part of the world just as much as with any other part of the earth's surface. We discuss U.F.O. activities in *U.F.O's And Their Mission Impossible* and (with John Weldon) in *Close Encounters: A Better Explanation*.

•

QUESTION: What is your opinion of Charles Berlitz and his book *The Bermuda Triangle*?

Charles Berlitz has written two books on the Bermuda Triangle, the second being *Without A Trace*. Larry Kusche (who wrote *The Bermuda Triangle — Problem*

*Solved*) has reviewed *Without A Trace* in the *Zetetic* Fall/Winter, 1977 edition, at pages 93 to 97. He makes the point that "most of the books on the current fiction best-seller list probably contain more truth than both of Berlitz's Triangle books put together."

He goes on to state, "What is not forgivable, however, is Berlitz's consistently inaccurate presentation of 'the facts,' time after time, in case after case." Kusche backs his claims by giving a number of specific examples of errors in Berlitz's books.

Similar criticisms are then given in a further review in the same volume by Philip J. Klass, who is a senior editor with *Aviation Week* and *Space Technology Magazine*. He gives examples of the reporting by Berlitz, and compares differences from those found by his own investigations.

•

### "Gas Giants"

QUESTION: Dr. Wilson, several years ago I read of evidence that gas giants (planets like Jupiter) had been discovered around other stars. So why do you say no other planets have been discovered around other stars?

If they are "gas giants" it does not mean that they are solid, as our *terra firma* is. We discuss this at length in a chapter in *Crash Go The Chariots*. Possibly you are referring to what is known as Barnard's Star.

The late Professor Fred Giles explained that in *Crash Go The Chariots* as follows:

"The only planet that we know for sure has life on it is the earth. One other star has been detected with a slight wobble, and this could mean that it has an invisible dark companion moving around it. Such a dark companion would make the star itself wobble. As a very slight wobble has been measured in relation to one star, some astronomers conjecture that the wobble is caused by a planet rotating around the star."

Professor Giles makes it clear that it is only conjecture as to whether there are other planets outside our solar system. We do NOT have the certainty of such planets, as Erich von Daniken puts forth.

•

## Mathematics and the Pyramid

QUESTION: Mr. von Daniken, is there any connection between U.F.O's (extra-terrestrial life)
and Egyptian technology such as mathematics
and pyramids they built?

I presume the question is referring to the remarkable mathematical, geometrical, etc., knowledge that is
obviously associated with the building of the Great
Pyramid in Egypt.  I elaborate this in another of my
books, *Gods In Chariots And Other Fantasies,* and part
of what follows comes from that book.

The early beginnings of so-called Pyramidology are
indirectly traceable to the engineers of Napoleon, but the
direct beginning comes from Charles Piazzi Smith.  He
invented special measuring instruments with which he
measured the Great Pyramid and its general environs.
He put out to the world that there were 36,524 "pyramid
inches" around the square at the base of the Pyramid,
and he went on to hypothesize that this was almost
exactly 100 times the number of days in a year.

At first sight this seems interesting, but the delusion
sets in when we realize that these "pyramid inches" are
the product of Smith's own mind, established by himself.
There is no empirical basis for such a measurement: it
is simply the standard that he decided.  Thus all calculations must be treated with great reserve, for the very
basis is unsound.

For a time the great archaeologist, Sir William Flinders Petrie, was taken in by these measurements.  His
own father had adopted them, and as a young man
Flinders Petrie was also taken in. That was long before he
became known as "the father of Egyptian archaeology."
When he himself went to Egypt, he soon showed that
Smith's measurements were seriously inaccurate, despite
his elaborate equipment.

Flinders Petrie actually disproved the whole basis of
Pyramidology, but the theories persist.  Even today many
people are taken in by measurements, calculations, and
prophecies that are based on error.  "Pyramidology"
should not be taken seriously.

Smith and his colleagues even put out the theory
that the British Standard Measurement for Volume was
also based on the Great Pyramid — that the British

Standard was based on the quantity of water that could be held by the empty stone sarcophagus found in the Pyramid.  This is quite ludicrous, for the sarcophagus had been shut up inside that artificial mountain of stone for many centuries, and to suggest it was the basis for a British measuring system is absurd.

Various religious movements have also taken up Pyramidology, and a number of prophecies have been made through the years, but they have a habit of not coming to pass.  A Great War was to break out in 1928, and Christ was supposed to return to earth in 1936.  The world should have come to an end in 1953.

Let me stress that such wrong prophecies and interpretations do not alter the fact that the Great Pyramid is a tremendous construction, even by today's standards.

Some very complex statistical calculations have been put forth, based on the Pyramid's measurements.  However, if one has enough figures to play with, he can produce all sorts of results.  This has been done with the pyramids, and with other famous buildings also.  One well-known example relates to the juggling of figures associated with the Temple of Artemis (Diana) at Ephesus: the "juggler" was supposedly able to estimate the diameter of the moon, the length of the lunar months, and the date when the building itself was built.

The statistics associated with the Great Pyramid have often been "juggled" in the same way, with various strange and nonsensical results.

I have a very interesting book called *The Great Pyramid. Its History and Teachings* by T. Septimus Marks, and it is dated to 1879.  It gives a whole series of dates supposedly associated with both the past and the future. However, it can now be shown that it is grossly in error. Thus it would not be agreed by archaeologists today that the Pyramid's date of foundation is 2170 B.C.: a date of about 2600 is accepted these days.

This table was put out by someone who believed very much in the Bible and Biblical prophecy, and he believed that the Pyramid fitted in with various aspects of the Bible.  He has some quite unacceptable chronological calculations, such as to suggest that the Pyramid was built by an older contemporary of Abraham.  He goes on to suggest that that contemporary was the King Melchizedec of Genesis Chapter 14, and that Melchizedec in turn was actually the patriarch Shem, one of the sons of Noah.

Many other criticisms could be made of the calculations, and of course the basic criticism is that the pyramid inch is itself a figment of Charles Piazzi Smith's imagination, as we have shown above.

It should be remembered that many thousands of facts could be associated with the movements of the earth, distances from one point to another, events that have taken place in the history of the world, and so on. Once figures are actually down, such as the measurements for the Great Pyramid, it is then possible to simply select whatever is required. What does not fit the particular theory can be conveniently put aside, because the figures themselves are set. Before long it is possible to come up with a great mass of calculations and imposing data.

As it is shown also in "The Case of the Ancient Astronauts" some of the calculations associated with the Great Pyramid are not as remarkable as is traditionally believed. Thus it is a relatively easy matter to gauge accurately the correct alignment to north, south, east and west. One method is to notice the rising point of a star in the east, trace it to its setting point in the west, then bisect the angle for either north or south. Similarly it is not difficult to get a true edge — men and poles can be used effectively. Nor is the height of the Pyramid when multiplied by 1,000 million equal to the distance from the earth to the sun. Such a calculation would give just over 91 million miles, whereas the sun's average distance from the earth is 93 million miles — which is not as accurate as would be expected from a space-travelling civilization.

We do not for a moment deny the remarkable nature of the pyramid constructions, but we are not at all impressed by many of the calculations and prophecies supposedly based on the mythical pyramid inch.

## Pyramid Power

Another point should be mentioned in passing: the so-called "Pyramid Power." There have been grossly exaggerated reports about razors being kept sharp, fruit ripened ahead of its time, people sleeping better in pyramid-shaped constructions, and so much more.

There have been two relevant reports in *Mechanics Illustrated* (April and September, 1977). The first (*The*

*Strange Truth About Pyramid Power*) gave the report of an inconclusive experiment that was construed by some researchers to suggest there was truth in the "Pyramid Power" concept.   The second (*The Crack in the Pyramid*) was a more careful analysis, and corrected the false conclusions stemming from the first investigation.

It could be argued that there is some occult power associated with the Great Pyramid, which is where the way-out stories originally came from.   However, the claims have gone beyond the Pyramid itself, for it is the SHAPE of the Pyramid that is now supposed to have special powers, plus proper positioning.

That is why the *Mechanics Illustrated* investigation is interesting.   The experiment with blunt razor blades was carried out under the conditions laid down by the "pyramiders" and the conclusion was that the "power" did not work.   At least in this case there was no scientific basis to the special powers supposedly associated with objects constructed in the same shape as the Great Pyramid.   The razor blades were as blunt as ever.

The article (by Bill D. Miller) points out a number of problems.   "Pyramiders" differ among themselves as to whether the pyramid angles should incorporate pi or phi.   If pi, the angle of the side to the base is 51 degrees 51 minutes; if phi, the angle would be 51 degrees 50 minutes.   In any case, as Miller points out, "no one can any longer say what the original angles were in the Great Pyramid, because its sides have been eroded."

Miller also shows that so many restrictions are laid down that it would be impossible to satisfy them all anyway — not near a fluorescent light, not under a window, not close to a radiator, not near a TV, or a radio . . . and so on.

Miller says, "You now probably understand why we've lost interest in pyramid power."

(So have we! We introduced this only in passing — it is a recent first cousin to Pyramidology.)

### The Pyramids of Egypt

Before we move on from the Pyramids, there are more "troublesome facts" to consider.

The facts about the pyramids are elaborated in Chapter 2 of *Crash Go The Chariots*, in Chapter 8 of *The Space Gods Revealed*, and Chapter 4 of *The Past Is*

*Human.* See also pages 61 to 74 of *Some Trust In Chariots.*

In *Chariots Of The Gods?* von Daniken tells us, "The pyramids and many other wonderful things shot out of the ground, so to speak." Also, "It seems obvious to me that the Pyramid cannot have been erected during a single lifetime" — and so Erich von Daniken suggests 664 years as his calculation for the time taken for their construction. Other points raised by von Daniken are:

The "heave-ho" method could not have been used to raise great stones. Because of the size of the stones, beings from beyond the earth must have been used in the building of the great pyramids. Wood was not available. There would not have been enough food for many thousands of laborers. There was no rope — and the pyramids were not simply burial places.

## Facts Again

1.   Egyptian culture did NOT suddenly "spring out of the ground." Its written records go back to the First Dynasty, about 3100 B.C. Hieroglyphic writing is based on everyday life in ancient Egypt, utilizing symbols of gods and temples, kings and priests, temples and palaces, homes, and clothing, and common utensils. Egyptian language was VERY earth-based, and NOT a sudden import from space! Even before the First Dynasty there was drainage of swamps, irrigation, growing of fruit and vegetables, making of pottery, and even international trade had commenced.

2.   Egyptian god-figures were very often in the form of birds, and not space-men. Horus had the symbol of a falcon, Thoth an ibis, and Ma'at a feather. Others were represented by animals, birds, reptiles and fish.

3.   The heave-ho method is still used to move great stones from excavations in Egypt. Wilson has witnessed this at Karnak.

4.   The average size of the Great Pyramid stones is $2\frac{1}{2}$ tons, not 12 tons as von Daniken has in his calculations. This would immediately reduce his 664 years to about 130.

5.   There were many pyramids, and about 40 mummified bodies have been recovered from the 80 pyramids so far known to have existed in Egypt (another 160 in Khartoum). The pyramids were burial places for Pharaohs and some noble people.

6.   An empty sarcophagus was found in the Great

Pyramid, at least indicating that death was associated with that building also. The sarcophagus was slightly wider than the room's entrance, so it clearly was there before the Great Pyramid was completed. The Pharaoh obviously took this aspect as being very important.

7.   The pyramids were always on the west side of the Nile, being associated with the setting sun. The departed Pharaoh was supposed to rejoin Ra the sun god on his daily journey, in "the chariot of the gods" (the sun itself).

8.   There was plenty of wood imported from countries such as Lebanon — Seneferu, the Pharaoh who was the father of Cheops for whom the Great Pyramid was built, actually tells of sending 40 ships to Phoenicia to import coniferous timber.

9.   Wooden sledges were used in ancient Egypt. One is depicted as early as 3100 B.C. on the Narmer Palette.

10.   Rope also was plentiful in early Egypt, mainly made from fiber or flax. Some was found at Saqqara, dating to about 3000 B.C.

11.   One famous scene in the tomb of the nobleman Djehutihotep depicts a statue stated to have weighed 60 tons, mounted on a wooden sled, and being pulled by 172 men. It is estimated that the statue was some 6.5 meters high, and it was dragged along by ropes.

12.   The pyramids actually were burial places, and followed along a pattern of mastabas. This was usually a rectangular stone structure, which was the earlier form of burial place for important people. The first pyramid was the Step Pyramid of Pharaoh Zozer, and it actually had six mastabas erected one on top of the other. (One is still beneath the sand.)

13.   The names of some Pharaohs are inscribed on blocks in various pyramids, and some have dates. The Pyramid of Meidum has different dates at points of construction.

14.   That pyramid is dated to about 2630 B.C., and is surrounded by enormous mounds of rubble. It collapsed, apparently because the design was inadequate — a typical human failure! They must have been rather poor space gods if von Daniken's hypothesis is correct!

15.   Pharaoh Seneferu (Cheops' father) is named twice on the Bent Pyramid at Dahshur. It actually had a date on the north-eastern corner stone, stating that it was built in the twenty-first year of Pharaoh Seneferu. Halfway up there is another date, this being the same

Pharaoh's twenty-second year.   Thus the time lapse between the two dates was under two years.

16.   As this famous "Bent Pyramid" is about two-thirds the size of the Great Pyramid, it is clear that nothing like 664 years was needed, as suggested by von Daniken.

17.   That Pyramid of Dahshur is dated to about 2600 B.C., and it is actually called the Bent Pyramid, having an abrupt change in angle from 54 degrees to 42 degrees. Apparently the design was changed to avoid a catastrophe such as that which had befallen the Pyramid of Meidum. It seems these astronaut gods could make mistakes, but were big enough to correct their mistakes! (Or maybe they were limited humans after all?)

18.   Various graffiti (wall scribblings) were found at the quarries from which stone for the Great Pyramid was taken.   One read, "The crew, Cheops excites love" — a very ordinary, earth-bound name for a gang employed by a known earthly king, and not a space-god!

19.   It is probable that the total period for the building of all the pyramids lasted for only about one century, this being the theory of physicist Kurt Mendelssohn, formerly of Oxford University.

20.   The ancient Greek historian Herodotus tells us that 100,000 workmen were employed in the building of the Great Pyramid, working in four shifts.   This figure might be exaggerated, but it does indicate that large numbers were used, and there is no reason whatever to suggest that astronaut help was employed.

21.   Herodotus says it took 20 years to build the Great Pyramid, after 10 years to build a causeway from the Nile — very different from von Daniken's 664 years.

22.   Another point relates to the levelling of the ground for the Great Pyramid.   It could have been done by filling the area with water, draining it away, and then the levels being determined by the depth of water at various points.

23.   Egypt had plenty of food for such large numbers. Cheops controlled both Upper and Lower Egypt, and the Nile Valley was very fertile.

24.   In the Cairo Museum there are copper saws and chisels, capable of cutting stone as hard as granite, to which von Daniken refers. (Most of the stone used was limestone, which is much softer.)

25.   In a quarry near Aswan a large block of granite

shows evidence of wedges having been used to facilitate splitting of rock — VERY un-astronaut-like implements!

In the film "The Case of the Ancient Astronauts" we were shown workmen using simple tools to break out a stone similar to those used in the Pyramid construction — it took about 15 minutes, with the rock splitting cleanly, along straight lines.  As the narrator in the film said, "In ancient Egypt ten men could easily have broken out about a dozen such stones in a week, and been able to maneuver them, without any great difficulty, from the quarry . . . 120,000 stones CAN be raised by 100,000 men in a year, given a good enough organization, something von Daniken ignores."

In that film von Daniken also made the point that he had never said in his book that the Pyramids were constructed by extra-terrestrials.  He had speculated that astronauts had left knowledge and tools to make the job easier.  As the narrator stated, "But we know what sort of tools they used — these simple copper chisels now on display in the Cairo Museum — hardly the advanced technology of space men!  Marks of some of those chisels are still on abandoned stones left at the quarries from where the stones were taken."

26.  Embalming was not taught by the astronauts to a bright young prince of Egypt (as von Daniken conjectures) because it pointed to eternal life with the gods. It was a way of preserving most, but not all, of the body. Some parts (including the brain) were not preserved. It would be a gullible prince who accepted embalming as a way of ensuring a continued astronaut-type life.  In the film referred to above von Daniken actually suggested the possibility of "the liquid of the brain" being available so that the astronauts could restore life to the mummified humans.  At that point the sound effects were used to make it sound as though one of the wizened mummies was giving a cynical chuckle.  Von Daniken's hypotheses really are absurd at times!

27.  The Pharaoh did not expect a visit from space, but hoped to take his journey in a very down-to-earth boat, such as the 143 foot long wooden boat found in 1954 in one of the boat pits in the temple complex of the pyramids at Gizeh.  It was a symbolic way of helping the king join the so-called Sun-god on its daily journey. Fancy that — a wooden boat, and not a space vehicle!

# Chapter 13:

# EASTER ISLAND ... STONEHENGE ... AND THE PIRI RE'IS MAP

### Easter Island

QUESTION: Why would the Easter Islanders place the statues where they did?

The answer is probably that they were pointing toward heavenly bodies. We have shown that many of these ancient people did associate their religious beliefs with the sun, the moon, and the stars. The Nazca lines and the Stonehenge stones are also probably associated directionally with heavenly bodies, and so are many South American relics from the past.

•

QUESTION: Dr. Wilson, why were the stone figures on Easter Island made? Why do they look off into space — return of astronauts?

Thor Heyerdahl says (in Ronald Story's *The Space Gods Revealed*, page 47) that "the local islanders re-called how their own ancestors had carved, transported, and erected the statues, which were raised as monuments for deceased kings and chiefs."

We have suggested (above) a possible reason why they "look off into space." It is also possible that they are looking across the SEA to the land where those ancestors came from. The three-masted ship depicted on one of their stone monuments, on a part buried until excavated by Thor Heyerdahl, indicates they knew about a sea voyage. There is no evidence of astronauts landing.

In any case, Erich von Daniken has said in this debate that he never said astronauts built the Easter Island statues! We agree they did not, but we wish Erich would make up his mind.

The Easter Island statues are discussed in Chapter 2 of *Crash Go The Chariots*, in Chapter 7 of *The Space Gods Revealed*, and, briefly, in *Some Trust In Chariots*. Thor Heyerdahl's *Aku Aku* is essential to this subject.

Once again we find that facts are troublesome things. Erich von Daniken has written, "The usual explanation that the stone giants were moved to their present sites on wooden rollers is not feasible in this case, either. In addition, the island can scarcely have provided food for more than 2,000 inhabitants. (A few hundred natives live on Easter Island today.) . . . Then who cut the statues out of the rock, who carved them and transported them to their sites? How were they moved across country for miles without rollers? How were they dressed, polished, and erected?"

He has the answer — the astronauts landed on Easter Island! — "An orally transmitted legend tells us that flying men landed and lighted fires in ancient times. The legend is confirmed by sculptures of tiny creatures with big, staring eyes."

The following points are relevant:

1.   Von Daniken says only "a few hundred" people lived on the island. Thor Heyerdahl, of *Kon Tiki* fame, puts the figure at about 7,000.

2.   Von Daniken sees it as an insuperable problem for the limited population to move the statues to their places of erection some miles away. Thor Heyerdahl estimated that about 1,000 men would have been required to haul the statues from the quarries to the sea, but only about 500 to transport them to their new home in those places where inclined ramps had already been prepared. The statues would have been taken up feet first and then the hat or top-knot (cut from a different type of stone) was dragged up the ramp and it also was placed in position.

3.   The Mayor of Easter Island and his team were descended from the group known as "the long ears." On payment of $100 from Thor Heyerdahl they showed the answer to three major questions. They demonstrated

   (a)  how the statues could be carved out of the volcanic rock;
   (b)  how they could be transported across the plain;
   (c)  how they could be erected.

4.   Von Daniken denies that the stone axes could have been used to make the statues, but hundreds of these stone axes were actually found in the quarry area. He invents a scenario whereby stranded intelligent beings are awaiting rescue, and so they relieve their boredom by constructing these statues. Stranded "gods" . . .

bored . . . using primitive stone axes?  One cannot help
wondering if von Daniken is serious.  Why would they
use such primitive tools, or how was it that they could
be successful with those tools and (he claims) native
Easter Islanders could not be?

5.  Thor Heyerdahl shows how the outline of a statue
could be etched into the volcanic rock by flaking along
the rock, then coming down about three centimeters and
repeating the process, and finally flaking out the rock in
between the two lines.  It was estimated that it would
take a year to complete the statue, which time was longer
than the European party planned to be on the island.
However, the point is that the technique had been
demonstrated to a recognized authority.  Despite his
objections about the method not being successful, von
Daniken actually acknowledges, "The stone tool theory
may be valid for some of the small statues."

6.  Thor Heyerdahl showed that the Mayor of the island
with 11 other men could lift one of the medium-sized
statues, by putting little stones under the statue as some
of the men pulled on poles that had been pushed against
the statue.  It was raised over a period of 18 days, with
the smaller stones being replaced by larger stones.  The
statue's weight was between 25 and 30 tons, and was
not one of the very smallest (as von Daniken has suggested).  Thor Heyerdahl tells how the men raised the
statue, and then had it fall exactly in an upright position
on the platform already prepared for it.

7.  Thor Heyerdahl also showed how the stone statues
could be moved across the plain.  He gave a feast to
about 180 local people, and then they took their places
on a long rope attached to the neck of one of the statues.
At the first attempt the rope broke, but it was doubled
and made fast again, and then it was able to be pulled
across the plain.  Eventually it moved "as quickly as if
they each were pulling an empty soap box."  They did
not haul the statue right across the plain, for they did
not want to take it from its actual site, but they had
shown that the statue could be moved by ordinary
humans, without calling in astronaut help. This was published before von Daniken's books were on the market.

8.  Von Daniken claimed (in *Gods From Outer Space*,
p. 116) that archaeologists all over the world had protested at Thor Heyerdahl's conclusions.  However, von

Daniken does not give any names of the archaeologists from all over the world who protested. This author (Wilson) has been associated with archaeologists for a quarter of a century and more, but does not know of the protests from all over the world.

9.   In that same context von Daniken has said that he was at first "quite prepared to cross an unsolved puzzle off my list as solved": it is a pity that he did NOT acknowledge that, and recognize that the so-called mystery HAS been resolved, instead of continuing to justify his dogmatically-held hypothesis, as he went on to do.

10.  Von Daniken also claimed that "Thor Heyerdahl made the natives hammer away for weeks with the old implements," but in actual fact the Mayor of Easter Island and six men carved out the contours of a new statue in three days, NOT a period of weeks.

11.  In "The Case of the Ancient Astronauts" Thor Heyerdahl points out that statues have been built by men exactly like us, with great ability to solve problems.

12.  In a letter published in The Space Gods Revealed, Thor Heyerdahl himself states, "With or without reason the feeling among those who could combat the world-sweeping hoaxes has been: Anyone stupid enough to take this kind of hoax seriously deserves to be cheated." Thor Heyerdahl goes on to say that von Daniken had "totally ignored these findings and publications [Thor Heyerdahl's reports on the properly conducted excavations.—Ed.] and concocted sheer nonsense to satisfy and entertain his space-hungry readers."

13.  Thor Heyerdahl goes on to state, "The general reader who cares to know has the right to be informed that there is not the slightest base of fact in what von Daniken writes about the origin of the giant statues on Easter Island. We know exactly how they were carved, where they were carved, why they were carved, and when they were carved. The last statues were carved about 1680 AD, when a civil war on the island interrupted all work in the image quarries of the extinct volcano Rano Raraku, near the eastern corner of the island." Heyerdahl further states in "The Case of the Ancient Astronauts," "This is a matter of not hundreds of years but more than a thousand years, that these statues were carved. By carving a few at a time, there is no problem at all to explain why (there are) close to a thousand statues."

14. Von Daniken says in *Gods From Outer Space*, "No one knows who the sculptures are supposed to represent. "Not even Thor Heyerdahl."

In his published letter in *The Space Gods Revealed,* Thor Heyerdahl states that "the local islanders recalled how their own ancestors had carved, transported, and erected the statues, which were raised as monuments for deceased kings and chiefs." (1st Ed., p. 47.)

15. As to the "hats" of the statues, von Daniken tells us in *Gods From Outer Space* that he had not found a convincing explanation, so he asks, "Had the islanders seen 'gods' with helmets and remembered the fact when it came to making the statues?" (p. 120). Thor Heyerdahl had already given the answer in *Aku Aku,* where he points out that the native name for the gigantic head decoration is *pukao,* and this means "topknot." This was in the shape of the usual headdress worn by Easter Island men at the time it was discovered (*Aku Aku,* p. 91).

We have already seen that Thor Heyerdahl states in his letter in *The Space Gods Revealed* that "the last statues were carved in 1680 A.D."

16. As Thor Heyerdahl points out, beings from outer space would need spaceships and accessories with incredible durability to resist the immense heat of friction encountered when descending through an atmosphere, but no fragment of such metal, plastic, or other fragment has been found where they supposedly landed, but only stone and bone tools.   They were certainly not brought from other planets.

17. One of the excavators with Thor Heyerdahl was Edwin Ferdon, now Associate Director of the Arizona State Museum.   In *The Space Gods Revealed* he states that it was not very difficult to carve the statues out of volcanic ash.   Water thrown on to the rock moistened its surface of the ash, and the surface became a little softer. He describes how the local people made two grooves with a keel in the middle, then knocked out the keel.

18.   Ferdon also makes the point that pollen studies have revealed that a much heavier cover of wood was on Easter Island in former times than was previously thought.   There were in fact large trees, and many species of plants that are now extinct locally.   As recently as in the eighteenth century Captain Cook had reported trees on Easter Island, and trees grow well on the island today.

Von Daniken claimed there was no proof the islanders had wood for rollers (*Gods From Outer Space*, p. 116).

19. The motif of the bird men is nothing to do with visits by spacemen. It had to do with a race to a nearby islet, to collect and bring back the first egg of the year laid by the sooty tern. The winner had special rights for the following year.

20. In answer to von Daniken's suggestion that only a few hundred people live on Easter Island today, Ferdon answered that about 1600 live there at present, and in earlier times there were probably far in excess of three or four thousand.

21. Furthermore, Easter Islanders are growing all the crops they need. Von Daniken claimed the food supply had always been short. (*Gods From Outer Space*, p. 116.)

22. Despite von Daniken's claims, the rainfall of Easter Island is about 45 to 50 inches per year.

We saw that it took 12 men 18 days to lift a statue that was between 25 and 30 tons in weight. Possibly other methods were used to raise the statues, but whatever method was used, Thor Heyerdahl's experiments have shown that the Easter Island inhabitants could certainly have carved them out of the volcanic stones, could have transported them across the plain, and could have raised them without using modern hydraulic equipment.

Certainly no visitors from outer space were needed to complete these projects!

•

## What About Stonehenge?

QUESTION: Mr. von Daniken, what was or is Stonehenge?

In the debate Mr. von Daniken stated that he had not elaborated on Stonehenge, though he had visited there. There is a chapter on Stonehenge in *The Chariots Still Crash* (Wilson — available from Signet Books, N.Y.), and we recognize that there are differing points of view. One strong possibility is that they were some sort of a giant astronomcial calendar, and we discussed that in *The Chariots Still Crash*.

It is relevant to point out that even bigger monuments than those associated with Stonehenge have been constructed with primitive tools, and the earlier arguments by some writers that Merlin's magic was supposedly activated, so that these stones could be brought from Wales, is of course nonsense. Erich von Daniken does include the Stonehenge monoliths as being juggled out of hills and valleys, as were other massive stones, and so to him the answer as to how they could be moved is apparently astronaut power.

At page 94 of *Gods From Outer Space* von Daniken states: "It even seems as if the ancient peoples took a special pleasure in juggling with stone giants over hill and dale. The Egyptians fetched their obelisk from Aswan, the architects of Stonehenge brought their stone blocks from south-west Wales and Marlborough, the stonemasons of Easter Island took their ready-made monster statues from a distant quarry to their present sites, and no one can say where some of the monoliths at Tiahuanaco come from. Our remote ancestors must have been strange people; they liked making things difficult for themselves, and always built their statues in the most impossible places. Was it just because they liked a hard life?"

He goes on to tell us that he refuses to think that the artists of our great past were as stupid as that, and then he further discusses the visits of space travellers. However, as larger monoliths were moved across great distances without astronaut help and without hydraulic power, once again we must reject Mr. von Daniken's way-out hypothesis.

●

## Two Mouths to a River

QUESTION: Erich von Daniken's map — you discussed about two mouths to a river. You said "No way." How come many rivers change course. Why couldn't this also be true?
("Clifford Wilson" was added at the end.)

This question was very badly written, and neither the Chairman nor Erich von Daniken could make sense of it. That was NOT their fault, as the question above has had punctuation added. It is not otherwise altered — though the Chairman read "man" for "map" — bad writing again. He thus thought it was a question to von Daniken, but it was really to Wilson.

At the debate Wilson commented that it appeared to be a reference to Elephantine Island on the Nile, which von Daniken claimed (in *Chariots Of The Gods?*) to be so named because it has, and always has had, the shape of an elephant. Wilson answers this in Chapter 6 of *Crash Go The Chariots*. Briefly, he shows that:

(i) the Greek word "elephantinos" does not mean "elephant" but "ivory," being a translation of the Egyptian word "Yeb," as the island was earlier called;

(ii) maps indicate that the island does NOT have the shape of an elephant today, and, in any case, if it were so shaped today this would argue more against von Daniken's claim than for it, for relatively small river islands may change their shape over long periods.

As shown above, the question is really dealing with another topic — the fact that the River Amazon is shown twice on the Piri Re'is map. However, it is not only that two mouths are shown for the Amazon, as they are, but that the River Amazon itself is shown a second time, some 300 miles separating the two delineations.

This is nothing to do with a river changing its course. It is a straight-out mistake which would not be the case with an aerial photograph.

### Facts About the Piri Re'is Map

See Chapter 6 in *Crash Go The Chariots*, Chapter 5 in *The Space Gods Revealed*, and Chapter 6 of *The Past Is Human*.

Another way in which facts are shown to be troublesome for von Daniken is in relation to this Piri Re'is map. According to von Daniken this was supposed to be part of a map of the world taken from a very great height (*Chariots Of The Gods?* p. 30). He claimed that this sixteenth century map was virtually identical with one taken from a spaceship hovering over Cairo, and urged that once certain juggling had taken place the map was "fantastically accurate." He then argues that the picture must have been taken from a high-flying aircraft or from a spaceship.

1. Piri Re'is himself has stated on the map in question that he consulted about 20 different earlier charts and eight "*Mappa Mundis*" (maps showing Jerusalem as the center of the world) as he prepared his own map. Piri Re'is tells of other authorities he had investigated, including a chart drawn by Columbus — possibly the legendary lost map of Columbus.

2. Thus the Piri Re'is map could only have been as accurate as the best of those from which he copied. It

contains a number of inaccuracies.

3. The River Amazon is shown twice on his map, with a third mouth of the Amazon shown at one point.

4. It has nearly a thousand miles of coast missing from the east side of America.

5. South America and Australia are joined to Antarctica. It has a number of extra islands in the Bahamas region.

6. This is explained by the fact that the Piri Re'is map was drawn in 1513, six years before Magellan sailed around Cape Horn, when he showed that America was separate from Antarctica.

7. There is no vast lake in the center of Spain, with rivers leading to the Atlantic and Mediterranean Oceans, as shown on the Piri Re'is map.

8. There is no network of lakes in Africa, including lakes in the Sahara, as shown on this map.

9. Von Daniken quotes Professor Charles H. Hapgood as suggesting that comparisons of modern photographs show that the originals of the Piri Re'is maps must have been aerial photographs taken from a very great height, but in his *Maps Of The Ancient Sea Kings* published in 1966 (pp. 37-38), Hapgood points to various errors made by Piri Re'is, and makes such statements as "The mis-labelling of Cuba also clearly shows that all he did was to get some information verbally from a sailor captured by his uncle, or from some other source, and then try to fit the information to a map already in his possession." Hapgood suggests that the original map might have come from the Byzantine Empire, and he then goes on to say that what we have "on the Piri Re'is map is a map of Cuba, but a map only of its eastern half."

10. Hapgood also shows that Piri Re'is has confused Japan with Cuba. (Elaborated further in *The Past Is Human*, p. 96.)

11. The Straits of Magellan and the Drake passage (800 kilometers) are missing.

12. Ronald Story makes the point that Hapgood did not suggest that the Piri Re'is map or any other ancient maps he studied were actually made from the air. Story says, "In reference to the Andes mountain range on the western side of South America, Hapgood states: '. . . the drawing of the mountains indicates that they were observed from the sea — from coastwise shipping'."

13. In his preface to his book Hapgood had theorized that "some ancient people explored the coasts of Ant-

arctica when its coasts were free of ice." (*Op. cit.*, preface.) However, this is very different from the implications that are made by Erich von Daniken. Hapgood suggested that the maps indicated that a lost civilization had advanced knowledge of navigation and map-making, but he did not suggest that the civilization had developed from space-gods, as von Daniken did.

14. Story points out that once again earlier authors such as Louis Pauwels and Jacques Bergier in *The Morning Of The Magicians* had put forward the same hypothesis about the Piri Re'is map.

15. The map was not discovered in the eighteenth century, as von Daniken suggests, but in the year 1929 when the old Imperial Palace of Constantinople was being converted into a museum. He himself corrected his mistake in his later book, *In Search Of Ancient Gods.*

16. In pages 14-16 of *Chariots Of The Gods?* von Daniken suggests that comparisons with modern photographs of our globe taken from satellites showed that the Piri Re'is originals must have been aerial photographs taken from a very great height — "Unquestionably our forefathers did not draw these maps. Yet there is no doubt that the maps must have been made with the most modern technical aids — from the air." In that same context he claims that Captain Arlington H. Mallery and Mr. Walters, cartographer of the U.S. Navy Hydrographic Bureau, stated that the maps were absolutely accurate, with the contours of North and South America, and even of the Antarctic, precisely delineated. We have seen that this is not able to be substantiated.

17. The maps were not always correctly drawn, and it is now recognized that the identification of Antarctica without its ice cover, as claimed by von Daniken, is erroneous. (See Gazeteer No. 14, August, 1966, Office of Geography, Department of Interior, Washington D.C., map of land mass below Antarctic ice-cap, reproduced in *The Space Gods Revealed*, p. 31.)

18. In *Playboy* magazine of August, 1974, at page 64, von Daniken actually retracts his argument about the Piri Re'is map, but he later repeats his conjectures about the map in *In Search of Ancient Gods.* There he states, "To me it is obvious that extraterrestrial spacemen made the map from space stations in orbit" (*In Search Of Ancient Gods*, p. 136.)

# Chapter 14

# HOW DO WE EXPLAIN PROGRESS, INTELLIGENCE AND GENETIC DIFFERENCES?

## From the Pyramids to the Gasolene Engine

QUESTION: Dr. Wilson, why was there a 6,000 year gap between the pyramids and a gasolene engine?

It is actually considered less than 6,000 years — it is about 4,600 years — but the question is a good one. The fact is that there do come bursts of activity, sometimes associated with particular inventions.

A very obvious example is the dramatic difference in achievements before World War 2 and those of the years following. Today the computer has dramatically altered our whole way of life. We do not need to think of the slowness of development over 4,000 years. Simply within one generation there have been amazing developments, but we do not suggest non-earth-centered help. Did the astronauts come down and give this knowledge in our generation? Of course not. However, in one generation great changes have taken place because of the computer, and there have been other dramatic developments.

Thus in one generation of air travel dramatic changes have taken place. It is a long way from the Wright Brothers to Neil Armstrong walking on the moon, but many people alive today are able to talk about both incidents as historical facts of their own lifetime.

Our point is, there are bursts of developmental activity, and these days there is serious argument that the Pyramid Age itself lasted only about a hundred years. It was a specific activity of a particular time, just as today there has been dramatic activity associated with air and space travel. The progress from Pharaoh Zozer's Step Pyramid at Saqqara to the Great Pyramid of Cheops is astounding. Perhaps even more astounding is the progress witnessed in so many fields in our own lifetime.

Actually the problem is one for von Daniken, and not for Wilson. If the astronauts suddenly "injected intelligence" so long ago (between 10,000 and 40,000 years ago, according to von Daniken), how come there was such slow progress for so long and then such remarkable acceleration in this generation? Von Daniken's hypothesis falls down badly! Again, it explains nothing.

•

### The Gaining and the Decline of Knowledge

QUESTION: Dr. Wilson, you mentioned "Grand Civilizations" 3,000 B.C. and their knowledge was lost until recently discovered. How is this decline of knowledge to be explained? Yet primitive tribes have maintained the passage of their culture through the ages.

Some things associated with ancient cultures have been lost, one specific example being the process of hardening bronze. However, in that particular case we now know the process, for it is demonstrated in the making of Japanese Samurai swords. There is nothing mysterious about the process, but it is a fact that the knowledge of it was lost for centuries.

Primitive tribes HAVE maintained culture, and have demonstrated remarkable intelligence and achievements, but they have not necessarily had the technological advancement known by Western civilizations. I do not regard so-called "primitive tribes" as being unintelligent. If their cultural backgrounds had been the same as those of Western peoples it is entirely possible that their present-day cultures would have been dramatically different from what they are. The same is true of Western people who have grown up in urban cultures in association with city life, etc. Left to themselves in the jungles, many developments would not have taken place.

•

QUESTION: Clifford Wilson, granting that early people are ingenious; from where did they obtain the knowledge necessary to even begin making the artefacts?

I personally accept that man was created in the image of God, as an intelligent being, able to undertake all sorts of activities. This would explain why the archaeological evidence strongly indicates that man was intelligent, and capable of undertaking projects involving technological skill, when he was in his settled civilization.

•

QUESTION: Mr. von Daniken, you say the gods deliberately mutated the beings on earth, and that we are now growing up towards the way they are. Where do you theorize or believe human-kind is leading to? Man's technology has GREATLY advanced within the past fifty years. Why was that advancement so slow in the past?

In the debate Mr. von Daniken likened this mutation hypothesis to the father-child relationship today. He conjectured that earth beings would follow the example of the space people. These latter know we will come out to them in space.

This appears to be a form of what might be called "pan-Universalism" of a very impersonal type.

Dramatic changes and leaps forward do take place from time to time, as with the Industrial Revolution. Such progress has no relationship to visits by astronauts.

(See also the answers to the following questions.)

•

QUESTION: Mr. von Daniken, if a society were capable of inter-stellar travel, why would they be bound to the use of relatively primitive facilities made of stone, that is, the "launch ramp," or be bound to using a re-entry system of runways? Surely they would be more advanced than to need these facilities. Please explain.

WILSON: Maybe Mr. von Daniken will explain some of these things in a later book, but he has not explained them satisfactorily in any of his current books, so far as Clifford Wilson knows. The question is a good one and highlights a major weakness in Mr. von Daniken's hypothesis.

•

### What Astronaut Gave us Radio?

QUESTION: Mr. von Daniken, what astronaut gave us steam power, or radio, or semi-conductor technology?

WILSON: Another good question! The fact is, of course, that these inventions simply illustrate that man is intelligent, ingenious, and has developed new technologies and methodologies over the centuries. He has done all this without astronaut help.

•

QUESTION: Mr. von Daniken, why didn't the ancient astronauts have a better propulsion system than puny inefficient "flames"?

WILSON: The so-called astronauts did not have "flames" — the example given by von Daniken of the "astronaut" at Palenque turns out to be a known ruler who lived in the seventh century A.D., and the "flames" were in fact a pictorial representation of the monster of the deep. It is similar to other known pictures.

However, it is true that if we were to meet astronauts of the type von Daniken hypothesizes, we would hardly expect them to use something involving such "puny, inefficient flames."

•

## Were Ancients All Stupid?

QUESTION: Mr. von Daniken, why must we assume ancient men were stupid? Are we so much smarter than they? What assumption and conceit!

WILSON: The questioner probably meant "presumption" rather than "assumption," as it is on the card. We have already referred to the journal *The Zetetic*, and the article by John T. Omohundro. At pages 62 and 63 of that article he has an excellent summary, making it clear that von Daniken does seem to think that ancient men were stupid, and that only Western moderns have highly developed intelligence.

He quotes from *Chariots Of The Gods?* at page 27 concerning primitive peoples, and makes the point that von Daniken's reasoning is that primitives cannot be Caucasians. At page 28 von Daniken argues that we cannot accept that there was a higher culture, or an equally capable technology, before relatively recent times. Von Daniken tells of "extraordinary things that could not have been made by any intelligence living at the time the tablets were written."

Omohundro has pointed out that von Daniken's reasoning is that only moderns have enough intelligence to be imaginative — this being based on the above quotation from page 49 of *Chariots Of The Gods?* concerning the *Epic of Gilgamesh.*

Von Daniken makes the point that the question of space travel did not arise a hundred years ago, and so our fathers and godfathers could not reasonably have had thoughts about whether our ancestors had visits from the universe.   As John T. Omohundro points out, this is just plain wrong.   There are plenty of writings well beyond a hundred years ago to show that men were indeed asking these questions.

At page 55 von Daniken talks about the Mayans and says that it is difficult to believe that their culture originated from a jungle people: thus the reasoning is that jungle people are dumber than most others.

Many social anthropologists would dramatically disagree with von Daniken at this point.   Studies of jungle people show they had a very advanced understanding of concepts which are different from those of "Western" culture, but are nevertheless highly complex, and demand considerable intelligence.

### "Anyone Civilized Before Us Cheated"

At page 63 von Daniken refers to Egyptian, Chinese, and Inca civilizations, and asks who put the idea of re-birth into the heads of these heathen peoples?   Thus the reasoning appears to be that heathen heads are "empty."

At page 65 he asks how the Egyptians could have had their highly developed civilization at such an early date.   Omohundro makes the telling point, "Anyone that was civilized before us cheated.   Whatever happened to the Honor Code?"   Undoubtedly von Daniken does not give enough credit to ancient people for being intelligent, ingenious, and able to adapt to various types of situations.   "Early" men were highly intelligent, as shown by their achievements.

As Graham Massey says in "The Case of the Ancient Astronauts": "On Easter Island as elsewhere von Daniken under-estimates the ability of people who to his eyes are primitive and unsophisticated."

In the same film Thor Heyerdahl stated, "Anybody who has lived among the so-called primitive people will know that their intelligence is exactly like our own, and their ability to solve problems I must confess is usually superior to that of modern man today."

•

## On Open-mindedness

QUESTION: Dr. Wilson, you have shown us that you are well educated and can recall and codify facts with great skill. But what about inspiration? Are objects from the past resembling equipment used in modern-day space travel merely co-incidental? If you allow only that mode of thinking I do not believe you study Shakespeare or any other area requiring open-mindedness.

Many of the so-called resemblances which Erich von Daniken presents are seen only by great stretches of imagination. Over and over again other possibilities would be acceptable, and the principle of Occam's Razor should be applied — to accept the simple explanation instead of others that are more difficult.

In any case, ancient people had all sorts of ideas as to the need to worship the gods of the heavens. Indeed, one of the great counterfeits shown in the Bible is this leaning towards heavenly bodies for false worship, when the true God of heaven was rejected.

Unfortunately, many of the so-called "co-incidences" between ancient and modern concepts of space travel, are not really co-incidences at all. One very good example has been demonstrated in this debate — that is, the figure of the ruler at Palenque in Mexico. He clearly is not a spaceman at all. Other "co-incidences" consistently demonstrate that man has changed little as to intelligence, ingenuity, and his search for answers regarding the supernatural.

As for studying Shakespeare, I can only say that my first degree included a great deal of Shakespeare study. In any case I believe I have shown in my extensive University studies, such as philosophy (and from very good secular universities), that I am certainly capable of open-mindedness in my thought patterns!

On the other hand, Mr. von Daniken would concede many points where he has been shown to be in error, if HE were open-minded.

THE WAR OF THE CHARIOTS

## Theories — Not Facts

QUESTION: Mr. von Daniken, is it not correct that your theories are based on interpretation of facts — your interpretation, not based on proven facts?

Unfortunately, this is entirely true. Unfortunately, also, Mr. von Daniken's interpretations are not always acceptable. An excellent survey which gives a very good answer to this question is in *The Zetetic*, the Journal of the Committee for Scientific Claims of the Para-Normal. In the Fall/Winter, 1976, edition there is an article by John T. Omohundro, entitled *Von Daniken's Chariots: A Primer in the Art of Cooked Science.*

Omohundro's argumentation against Mr. von Daniken is very strong. He sees "von Daniken's approach as a warped parody of reasoning, argumentation, as well as a vigorous exercise in selective quotation, misrepresentation, and error — based on ignorance (presumably, if it is not intentional fibbing)." (Page 59.)

He suggests that Mr. von Daniken misrepresents the things to be argued against, such as in his characterizations of archaeology and anthropology, which are abysmal. He tells us that von Daniken's critics "are nearly unanimous in accusing him of misrepresenting or failing to understand even the rudiments of geology, mythology, psychology, chemistry, astronomy, and physics" (page 60).

Omohundro suggests another technique used by Mr. von Daniken is the red herring, and that "the object is to confuse the reader by introducing an extraneous issue so that he will not catch you on your main point" (page 61). That is well put! Omohundro gives various examples, and suggests concerning these von Daniken writings, "these comments are quite irrelevant to his arguments and serve only to glaze the reader's critical judgment" (page 62).

He goes so far as to say, "Von Daniken's book is a virtual gold mine of logical fallacies, implications by innuendo and rhetorical questions, and failures to apply Occam's Razor."

Occam's Razor applies to the concept of taking the simplest explanation where two or more possible explanations are put forward. He further quotes *Book World* as saying, "To check his 'facts' would take months of research, since he never cites his authorities" (page 65). He points out that "his highly selective choice of what to introduce as data follows absolutely no discernible criteria."

We agree.

●

### Ancient Voyagers and their "Space Travels"

QUESTION: Mr. von Daniken, I have heard it mentioned that there are theories of these ancient voyagers returning to earth. The ideas for these theories were written in ancient documents, inscribed on tablets, etc. Do you know anything about these theories?

To answer this would need an elaboration on Mr. von Daniken's various books. He has a great deal to say about myths and legends of ancient peoples. He claims that sometimes these are in fact records about space travellers and their journeys to earth. Wilson does not accept most of the mythologies referring to spacemen and their journeys in this way — e.g., the "chariots of the gods" in Egypt is merely an expression referring to the sun. The Egyptians believed that their Pharaoh rejoined the sun on his death, and so made a daily journey across the sky. Most ancient mythologies would hardly be an acceptable basis for a serious theory of origins.

●

### About Creation

QUESTION: Dr. Wilson, can you absolutely account for man's evolution from age to age with reason and intelligence? In other words, how did man become intelligent?

Mr. von Daniken has made it clear in his latest book, *According To The Evidence*, that he does not accept Darwinian evolution. He gives a great mass of statistical information to show how impossible it is. Much of that material I accept, for as a Creationist I believe that man was created intelligent, as taught in the Bible.

My other field (of archaeology) has long ago taught me to have great respect for the teachings of that Book — that would be my approach even if I were not a committed Christian. The evidence for the acceptability of the Bible as a remarkably accurate source Book is overwhelming.

### Von Daniken Rejects Darwin

As I have said above, Mr. von Daniken himself denies all possibility of evolution according to the basic Darwinian hypothesis. He elaborates the necessity for creation — in his case it is a series of creations actually, associated with so-called "gods" from other planets.

If there is to be an act of creation, it is far more acceptable to come to the Biblical record than to the nonsensical association of genes and chromosomes in ways that are simply opposed to fact, as propounded by Mr. von Daniken. There is still no other acceptable explanation for man's creation, and for his intelligence, than the fact that he was created by the one true omnipotent God Who is revealed in the Bible.

●

QUESTION: Mr. von Daniken, why genetic manipulation? Why not a naive Adam and Eve?

WILSON: Yes — the concept of God creating Adam and Eve is very much easier to accept than the sort of genetic manipulation that Mr. von Daniken postulates.

●

QUESTION: Mr. von Daniken, look at the digestive system of humans — LESS able to handle meat than would be expected of a carnivore. We descendants ought NOT to be eating all of the planet's food. Our native protein, etc., was easier to digest!

WILSON: It is indeed true that some aspects of the higher developments in man are superior to those of so-called lower beings, and some are actually inferior. This is not surprising, for God the Creator had a blueprint, and if it suited Him to have so-called lower forms having higher abilities in a particular area, that was His business. It raises no problem to the believer in creation. It raises great problems, as is implied in this question, to the believer in chance evolution as the total explanation for man's development.

### A Famous Trial

QUESTION: Dr. Wilson, do you support Clarence Darrow or William J. Bryant in *The Scopes Trial?*

This question is interesting, for it is really asking am I a Creationist or an Evolutionist. I am a Creationist — that has become quite clear during the debate, and also in my books.

However, it is also interesting because in the trial referred to in the question, much was said about the writings of Charles Darwin. We said above that in *According To The Evidence* Erich von Daniken makes it abundantly clear that he deliberately rejects Darwinian evolution, declaring (with good evidence) that it is statistically impossible and logically unacceptable. It would be interesting to put the question to Mr. von Daniken instead of to Dr. Wilson! (Actually the trial itself got off on to a number of side issues dragged in by the defence lawyer, William J. Bryant.)

●

### When were the Visits?

QUESTION: Mr. von Daniken, if humans were genetically tampered with by extra-terrestrial "astronauts," when approximately (years ago) did this occur? How do you account for written historical records previous to this "injection of intelligence" into the apes of planet earth?

WILSON: In his writings Mr. von Daniken gives a series of dates, not always consistently. It is indeed true that recovered records demonstrate that man was an intelligent being before some of the dates associated with these so-called visits of gods from space. Mr. von Daniken now suggests three dates for "astronaut" visits:
      (i) between 10 and 40,000 years ago;
     (ii) in "pre-Sumerian times" about 4,000 B.C.; and
    (iii) in Biblical times.
When he first debated me about four years ago it was only once. In Biblical times we have Moses (about 1400 B.C.), Ezekiel (about 600 B.C.), and then, later, we also have the Palenque "astronaut" about 680 A.D. What an amazing condensation of 2,000 years into one visit!

### Zombies to Geniuses?

QUESTION: Clifford Wilson, zombies to geniuses? Cheap! Real cheap!

At page 13 of *Gods From Outer Space,* von Daniken says, "So far I have not been fortunate enough to hear an explanation of the origin of intelligence in man that is even tolerably convincing." The answer, so far as Erich von Daniken is concerned, is that man as an intelligent being has been created by his astronaut god figures. There had been a deliberate breeding by the beings who had reached us from Mars, or other places, for von Daniken has changed his conjectures on this at various times. He has this breeding process taking place by sexual intercourse, by artificial fertilization, by the manipulation of the genetic code, or by artificial mutations.

In *The Space Gods Revealed* Ronald Story has an interesting summary: "I will not elaborate on the problems this kind of limitation might impose on the mating process. Besides the unlikelihood that the physical form of von Daniken's interplanetary visitors would allow such a mating, a similarity in genetic make-up, which would be a biological necessity, even for artificial insemination, is unlikely in the extreme. Not only would the chromosomes of the two species have to be of the same shape and number, but their genes would have to be in the same basic arrangement and be located on corresponding chromosomes. This poses yet another flaw in the theory: if the chromosome number, and the arrangement of genes on the chromosomes, are similar enough to allow fertilization and viable offspring, the two beings would already be of the same or closely related species.

"As is his way, von Daniken dismisses a troublesome problem with a rhetorical question. Acknowledging that a cross between man and animals is considered impossible, he asks, 'But do we know the genetic code according to which the chromosome count of the mixed beings was put together?' Here he really betrays his ignorance of genetics. The genetic code has no direct bearing on chromosome count; it codes genetic information by which proteins are synthesized in the cell.

"Von Daniken's superficial understanding of modern genetics is further revealed by his misuse of the terminology. When scientists perform genetic surgery, or genetic engineering, which is what von Daniken's space-gods apparently undertook, they do not manipulate the genetic code, but manipulate the DNA, or deoxyribonucleic acid, which is the chemical name for the basic genetic material.

"There is simply no reason to suspect what von Daniken calls an artificial mutation, or tinkering of any kind in the evolution of man. And even if there were, a classic philosophical problem would arise. If the astronaut-gods are necessary in explaining the origin of human intelligence, then other gods would be necessary to explain the origin of their intelligence, and so on, *ad infinitum*. Therefore this explanation renders the astronaut-gods superfluous."

I have discussed this material with Ronald Story, and he has given me permission to use it. I do not think that the point needs further elaboration. Story has given some highly relevant material as to the impossibility of von Daniken's basic hypothesis.

It is von Daniken's conjecture that is "cheap, real cheap," as per the question. Probably that is what the questioner meant anyway.

•

### Man Is Earth-bound After All!

QUESTION: Mr. von Daniken: Why, in stating your overall theory, do you say man, **as a species intricately bound up with the earth, as a species with a natural and social evolution that follows discernible earthly patterns,** underwent fundamental biological and psychological change at the hands of his visitors? Doesn't the archaeological and evolutionary evidence contradict **this**? Haven't we prospered upon the earth precisely because we are descendants of the earth and her patterns?

WILSON: I'm afraid Mr. von Daniken would have to disagree with a number of your points, for in his latest book, *According To The Evidence*, he makes it clear that he does not accept an evolutionary pattern. He rejects Darwin and evolution as such.

In my own cognate field of archaeology, it is certainly true that "the archaeological evidence contradicts" various arguments put forward by Erich von Daniken.

As for our prospering on the earth because we are descendants of the earth and her patterns, while I do not agree with some of the basic philosophy of this question, it certainly is true that man is earth-bound, using the products of earth, and at no point can we point to space materials that have helped man in his progress or are continuing to be used by man. We cannot even point to their debris — and there is plenty of that on the moon now!

●

### Where did Blacks and Whites Come From?

QUESTION: Mr. von Daniken, how do you explain the evolution of blacks, whites, and other races found on our planet with your theory of being "seeded" by visitors from another planet?

WILSON: One is almost tempted to be facetious and elaborate the idea that maybe Mr. von Daniken's visitors found a colony of albion apes on one of their visits!

To be serious, the most remarkable outline of the early divisions of mankind is found in the Table of Nations, at Genesis Chapter 10 in the Bible. The late Professor William Foxwell Albright, one of the truly greats of archaeology, said this about it:

'It stands absolutely alone in ancient literature without a remote parallel even among the Greeks . . . 'The Table of Nations' remains an astonishingly accurate document . . . (It) shows such remarkably 'modern' understanding of the ethnic and linguistic situation in the modern world, in spite of all its complexity, that scholars never fail to be impressed with the author's knowledge of the subject."

Other nations, such as the Greeks, had stories as to the origins of peoples, but they are clearly mythological. The Bible "Table of Nations" is unique, and is another strong pointer to the fact that Bible records stand alone among the documents of ancient times.

Probably the above material gives my point of view as to the origin of nations, with them all ultimately coming from the creation of one pair by Almighty God.

As to the specific point about "black" and "white" races I am unqualified to answer the question except in the most general terms. However, the following comment by Professor William C. Boyd is relevant:

"We should not be surprised if identical genes crop up in all corners of the earth, or if the over-all racial differences we detect prove to be small. We do not know the total number of gene differences which mark off a Negro of the Alur tribe in the Belgian Congo from a white native of Haderslev, Denmark. Glass has suggested that the number of gene differences even in such a case is probably small. Besides a few genes for skin colour, he thinks that there may be a dominant gene for kinky hair and a pair or two of genes for facial features. He considers it unlikely that there are more than six pairs of genes in which the white race differs characteristically from the black. This estimate errs somewhat on the small side, in the opinion of the present writer. Probably, however, it is of the right order of magnitude, and any outraged conviction that the difference between the two races must be much greater than this, which some persons might feel, is likely to be based on emotional, rather than rational, factors." (In *Genetics And The Races Of Man*, pp 200f.)

Thus Professor Boyd makes it clear that there is not so much difference between the races after all. As the apostle Paul says in the New Testament, "God has made of one blood all nations of men to dwell on all the face of the earth" (Acts 17: 26). Professor Boyd goes on to say:

"An inherited difference becomes vital as marking off a race only when someone chooses to treat it as vital . . . A Semitic nose or a black skin is no more significant . . . than a head of flaming red hair."

Much has been written as to differences brought about by climate and hereditary factors, and it seems likely that when combined these could well be a sufficient explanation. Why should not those relatively insignificant hereditary factors be traced to the sons of Noah? (Interestingly enough, it is the dark races who have an additional genetic characteristic to give them protection against the sun.)

**Chapter 15:**

# QUESTIONS ABOUT JESUS, THE FLOOD, AND BIBLE RECORDS

In this chapter we have brought together the questions asked at North Dakota about Jesus, the Flood, Ezekiel, and the reliability of the Bible. In passing we see something of von Daniken's attitude toward spiritism.

•

### "Was Jesus a Spaceman?"

QUESTION: Mr. von Daniken, was Jesus Christ a spaceman?

WILSON: In *Chariots Of The Gods?* (page 121), von Daniken allies Jesus Christ with Mohammed and Buddha, as three of those whom people in touch with U.F.O's would claim to have messages from. He is reflecting against religious cranks, and is not saying Jesus was an astronaut at that point.

Erich von Danikens' concept of Jesus is very different from the orthodox Christian viewpoint. He does not accept that He was the Son of God in the sense that Christians do.

This is made clear in his writings. We read such things as, "even Jesus, the Master, did not believe in miracles . . . but He knew the effect of suggestion!" (*Miracles Of The Gods*, page 167.) Thus we learn that the woman who says, "If I may but touch His clothes I shall be whole" (Mark 5: 28) was merely a demonstration that "the Nazarene KNEW nothing about the mechanism of auto (or hetero) suggestion, but he had a good idea of their miraculous effects."

The Christian believer will never go along with Erich von Daniken's assessment of Him Whom they worship as the Son of God.

### Life from Dead Matter

In the middle of all this, in that same book, he sandwiches strange material such as the fact that " 'LIFE' clearly developed from 'dead' matter, there is no longer the slightest doubt about that" (page 172). (Well!) This of course is dramatically different from what he tells us in his later book, *According To The Evidence*, where he has a great deal to say against Charles Darwin and also against the hypothesis of evolution.

## Contact with the Dead?

In various other ways he opposes orthodox Christian teaching.  For instance, if there is any doubt that von Daniken believes in contact with "the other side," this doubt is removed in *Miracles Of The Gods* at page 181 and the following pages.  He talks about what happens to consciousness after death, and tells us that it has already been brought to light that the consciousness of the dead is by no means "dead."  He talks about space people who recover from such experiences, and tells us that they perceive the other world as being a place of harmonies and colors, with countless consciousnesses communicating with each other, carrying on conversations, and even seeing acquaintances and sharing memories with them.

Those who have returned from the other side, according to von Daniken, have found this mortal life distasteful, and even "repugnant" (page 182).  They claim that everything was infinitely more beautiful "over there" (page 182).

He even informs us how voices can be hunted down in one's own home at little expense, and tells how anyone can call on dead persons (or spirits) to announce themselves (page 183).  He tells how different languages can be recorded by such contact, and that there are different voices, with sounds, words and fragments of sentences that are hissed or sometimes only whispered (page 184).  He explains in some detail how to be associated with this sort of "communication" as he tells us that the hunt for voices from the other side is still continuing (p. 185).

He elaborates experiences where people have been under hypnosis and have told of early experiences in their own lifetime, and then of other existences before birth.  He includes the well-known case of Mrs. Ruth Simmons, who was hypnotized by Morey Bernstein, then began to talk under the name of Bridey Murphy.  She gave many remarkable facts about the life of a Bridey

Murphy who had lived in Ireland about the middle of the nineteenth century.

This is not the place to elaborate the facts associated with supposed communication with the dead, and the imitation and counterfeiting that thereby takes place. This author (Wilson) has written at length about this in *The Occult Explosion*, and there are many other books dealing with the subject. Our point is that von Daniken is endorsing these practices, and this is all part of his hypothesis concerning the so-called space gods. He suggests that these supposed energies from the 'other world' can communicate with men living today, and this is dangerous in its Satanic overtones. It is blatant spiritism which the Bible clearly warns against, and which every wise person should reject.

Von Daniken puts some of this subtle deception out in a way that at first seems acceptable to the unwary. He makes it clear that he is suggesting that visions do exist (page 212), and that "apparitions announce themselves to visionaries when the latter are in a state of hypnotic compulsion and what I can only call helplessness" (page 213).

He suggests that visions are the special form of communication that should be developed so that interstellar communication will become possible (page 214).

### "He Becomes a Medium"

Von Daniken makes it very clear that he is indeed talking about concepts that are opposed to orthodox Christian teachings. He elaborates at great length about the privilege of having visions, and then tells us, "The situation seems clear to me. EXTRA-TERRESTRIAL IMPULSES cause the brain to produce visions. The vision itself is NOT extra-terrestrial; it reveals the image desired by the visionary" (page 231). He then tells us that the Hindu will see Brahma, and the Catholic will see Jesus, the "blessed virgin," angels, and saints. Every recipient of a vision reproduces the religious world of ideas familiar to him, according to von Daniken. He goes on to say that "at the moment the visionary comes into the sphere of an extra-terrestrial impulse field he becomes a medium" (p. 232.) He then makes the illuminating statement, "He cannot avoid the impulses which reach his brain."

A medium . . . controlled by forces he cannot resist. This is one of the frightening implications of spiritism.

The Bible teaches that it is Satanic. These points are elaborated at great length by Weldon and Wilson in *Close Encounters: a Better Explanation*. Beings in U.F.O's, and entities associated with other manifestations of the occult, do indeed take over a human brain. The only way of deliverance from such control is the greater power, that of Jesus Christ Who died on a cross to give man deliverance and freedom. It is still true that if the Son shall make you free, you shall be free indeed.

Von Daniken ends the chapter, and his book, with a statement concerning visions that great men get from the extra-terrestrials. He tells us, "THEY ARE THE ONES I BELIEVE IN." Clearly, von Daniken does not accept that Jesus is the Son of God, in the Christian sense. In *According To The Evidence* he writes openly of his own supposed contact with the dead Jules Verne.

Some of the arguments against the Person of Jesus Christ put forward by Erich von Daniken in *Miracles Of The Gods* are blasphemous, and in fact we prefer not to discuss them.

However, we can say that the supposed "clear agreements" between the teachings of the Essenes of Dead Sea Scroll fame and those of Jesus are not as close as von Daniken suggests. (*Miracles Of The Gods*, pp. 76 ff.) There are similarities, for the Essenes were a sect of the Jews and had a Jewish background. Jesus was a Jewish teacher, and it would be strange if He did not utilize background common to Himself and to the Essenes. Actually we elaborate these differences and similarities in Chapter 13 of *That Incredible Book — The Bible* (Wilson). There we quote A. N. Gilkes from *The Impact Of The Dead Sea Scrolls*:

"It would be easy to continue the list of resemblances in idea and in phrasing . . .

"But we must also strike a balance by pointing out once more the enormous gap between Essene and Christian . . . The whole vast range of specifically Christian thought — the whole difference which Christ makes — separates the two."

The great differences are well summarized by Gilkes:

"These differences between Jesus and 'the Teacher,' between Christian and Essene, go very deep and very wide. Nothing less than the word 'chasm' could describe the difference between what the Gospels

tell us of the life and personality of Jesus, and the
little we know of the Teacher's. For the Christian, too,
there stretches and shines between them the whole
majesty of the Incarnation. There is no suggestion
that the Teacher was a divine being during his time
on earth or that he died for others; there is not a word
about redemption, about his cross and passion, or 'his
precious death and burial, or his glorious resurrection
and ascension, and the coming of the Holy Ghost'."

The teachings of Jesus are greatly superior to those
of the Teacher of Righteousness, the leader of the Dead
Sea community at Qumran.

•

### "The Sons of God Saw the Daughters of Men"

QUESTION: Mr. von Daniken, there is a passage in Genesis which suggests that the sons of
gods saw that the daughters of men were fair
and they mated. Could this be a reference to
astronauts, and do you refer to this passage in
your writing?

Answer: The reference is to "sons of God" seeing "the
daughters of men" at Genesis Chapt. 6. Mr. von Daniken
discusses this passage in Ch. 4 of *Chariots Of The Gods?*
(Wilson also discusses it in his book, *In The Beginning God,* at Chapter 8.)

Some Bible scholars teach that the "sons of God"
referred to at Genesis Chapter 6 were fallen angels, but
I believe this is opposed to the teachings of Scripture
as to the angels being without sex. At Matthew 22: 30
our Lord refers to the future state where believers neither
marry nor are given in marriage, but are as the angels
of God in heaven.

Possibly the "sons of God" referred to at Genesis
6: 2 were the godly line of Seth, while the "daughters
of men" were from the ungodly line of Cain.

The fact of giants in the earth is not surprising —
if the Bible account is accepted the race was much
purer, and therefore physically healthier than now.

The word used for "giants" is used again in relation
to the inhabitants of Canaan at the time of the conquest
by Joshua. Another point is that the expression "these
beings took to themselves wives" is the same expression
that is used throughout the Old Testament for the usual
marriage relationship. It does not refer to a casual sex

act, but to the continuation of marriage as such. This seems to suggest that these were not fallen angels, but two different groups of humans coming together. We have suggested above that these were the godly line of Seth and the ungodly line of Cain.

However, there are many conservative scholars who hold that the "sons of God" referred to here were fallen angels. "Sons of God" is sometimes used in reference to angelic beings, as in the story of Job.

Another possibility is that "the sons of God" were actually kings of old. My friend and colleague David Livingston heads up *Associates for Biblical Research* in Philadelphia. He has a book in preparation dealing with early man, and he has dug up (not literally!) a great deal of information to show that "sons of God" could refer to early kings. Sometimes they took this as a title.

Thus we have three different interpretations, each put forward by Bible-believing scholars. Where there are legitimate differences of opinion I personally am not dogmatic.

One other point should be added. In *Close Encounters: A Better Explanation* John Weldon and I give documented evidence of APPARENT sexual activity between U.F.O. occupants and humans. We identify such entities as Satanic emissaries, on good academic grounds. However, we know of no convincing evidence of an offspring from the sexual union of a demonic being and a human. Other types of relationships with a "demon-possessed" person are another matter.

The passage in Genesis clearly refers to offspring (verse 4), and to this author that seems to rule out the interpretation of demons cohabiting with women of earth.

### The Flood

QUESTION: Dr. Wilson, in your research how many different accounts of the great flood have you found? Where was it? How great an area did it cover?

Over 300 traditions of the flood are known, with more than 30 written records recovered. The remarkable similarity of many of the traditions, right around the world, suggests that it was world-wide. The Bible account of the flood is still the best known, and though

there are similarities between it and some of the other
accounts such as those of the Sumerians, the Bible
account appears to be the original. If that is so, it took
place in the general area of the Fertile Crescent initially,
with the ark landing on Mount Ararat. This would mean
that man had a new start in the general area of Turkey,
with civilizations spreading out progressively from that
area. This and other questions are elaborated in my book
*In The Beginning God.*

Mr. von Daniken also touches on the flood. At one
point he refers to the *Epic of Gilgamesh* (in *Chariots Of
The Gods?*). He asks if it could not have originated with a
South American culture, and from there found its way
into Egypt, into the hands of Moses, and so it could
have become basic to the writings of Genesis and Exodus.
This is absurd — Moses lived about 2,000 years BEFORE
the culture Mr. von Daniken talks about, yet he tells us
(wrongly — at page 41) that the Epic is "much older than
the Bible," and on the same page he asks, "Or does
the whole account in Exodus come from the *Epic of
Gilgamesh*? Even that is possible." On page 45 he says,
"It is also clear that the main thread of the Epic of
Gilgamesh runs parallel to the Biblical Book of Genesis."
At page 49 he asks, "Is it possible that the *Epic of
Gilgamesh* did not originate in the ancient East at all,
but in the Tiahuanaco region? Is it conceivable that
descendants of Gilgamesh came from South America and
brought the Epic with them?"

## It is a Conglomeration!

What more shall we say? It is a conglomeration!
Here is one more quote from the tangled mess at page
50: "Moses grew up at the Egyptian court and certainly
had access to the venerable library rooms . . ." He
goes on to hypothesize "the young Moses" finding the
Epic there and that he "adapted it for his own ends,"
"then the Sumerian story of the flood, and not the Biblical
one, would be the genuine account."

In *That Incredible Book: The Bible* (Wilson) we
quote Professor W. F. Albright as stating that the Biblical
account is the oldest known, and NOT the *Epic of Gilgamesh* as von Daniken suggests.

Many of von Daniken's statements are pathetic, as
the following few points show:

(i)   There are many hundreds of years between Moses and the South American civilization at Tiahuanaco (Moses was the earlier);

(ii)  There is confusion between Tiahuanaco and early Sumerian culture;

(iii) The *Epic of Gilgamesh* is NOT parallel to Genesis. In the *Epic of Gilgamesh* there is a corrupted version of the Flood, but the Flood story is only a relatively small part of the Genesis record;

(iv)  The bulk of Genesis gives the record of Abraham and the early Hebrews — nothing to do with the Gilgamesh Epic;

(v)   Exodus is the history of the Israelites in Egypt, and their moving out towards Canaan — it is nothing whatever to do with the Babylonian Epic.

Much more could be said. The straight-out mistakes and misunderstandings associated with this one Epic should be enough to rule out the "scholarly" credibility of Erich von Daniken. His writings abound with such errors. He confuses so much that it is almost incredible.

### The Wrong Sargon — and Carl Sagan

Another example is in *According To The Evidence* (page 113), where he tells of a great library of the Akkadan King Sargon the Great, who lived about 2400 B.C. No such library has been recovered, but some elaborate records were recovered from the palace of the much later Assyrian Sargon II (much further north in Assyria). This later Sargon is referred to at Isaiah 20: 1 and it is probable that von Daniken is confusing the two rulers. There is about 1700 years between them.

Professor Carl Sagan of Cornell University says in his foreword to *The Space Gods Revealed*, "I know of no recent books so riddled with logical and factual errors as the works of von Daniken." Wilson agrees!

●

### "Extracting" Historical Bits

QUESTION: Mr. von Daniken, why do you extract historical bits while disregarding the theological framework?

Unfortunately von Daniken does not even quote historical aspects in a way that is acceptable to scholarship. He seldom gives references to his source material, and the uninformed reader does not know that Mr. von Daniken can be challenged over and over again.

Thus he makes statements about the Dead Sea Scrolls that are plain wrong as to his basic facts, as well as his methodology. At page 60 of *Chariots Of The Gods?* he refers to "hitherto unknown texts" supposedly made recently, when the Dead Sea Scrolls texts were found at Qumran, this being especially a reference to the already-known *Apocalypse of Moses*.

The fact is that this has been a known text since the fourteenth century A.D. It is accepted as being typical pseudepigraphic literature that Jewish writers produced in early Christian times. By "pseudepigraphy" is meant a literary form whereby an authoritative, earlier name is given to a later work. This test was known long before the modern recovery of the Dead Sea Scrolls.

## "Without Actually Consulting Exodus"

Another example of von Daniken's "extracting historical bits" is the way he refers to the Ark of the Covenant which Moses had built: "Without actually consulting Exodus, I seem to remember that at times the ark was surrounded by flashing sparks," he tells us (pp. 40, 41 *Chariots Of The Gods?*). However, you can consult Exodus from cover to cover and you will find no mention of flashing sparks associated with the Ark of the Covenant. Von Daniken conjectures Moses communicating with God by a two-way system. This is nonsensical, and to say the least it is very, very careless. (We elaborate this in *Crash Go The Chariots*.)

## That "Electrified" Ark

This we discuss in Ch. 3 of *Crash Go The Chariots*.

The incident of the supposedly electrified Ark of the Covenant is recorded in the Bible, at 2 Samuel 6. A man named Uzzah grabbed the Ark and died. Von Daniken accepts the story and says, "Undoubtedly the Ark was electrically charged!" (*Chariots Of The Gods?* page 40.)

Some of the relevant facts are as follow:
1. Von Daniken says, "Without actually consulting Exodus, I seem to remember that the Ark was often surrounded by flashing sparks. . . .

(Not in Exodus!)

2.    ". . . And that Moses made use of this 'transmitter' whenever he needed help and advice" (pp. 40-41).
(Moses was in touch with God before the Ark was made.)
3.    On Melbourne (Australia) radio von Daniken was unable to say where in America a model of this "dangerous" ark had been constructed, as had been reported.
4.    The Ark's construction as given in Exodus meant there was virtually only one metal plate: thus there was not one negative and one positive.
5.    Thus the conditions needed for a condenser were not met — there were not 2 pieces separated by an insulator.
6.    The whole Ark was covered exactly by the Mercy Seat, and no one could have put his hand inside, even if there had been two plates inside (which there weren't).
7.    A condenser needs to be charged — where would Moses have plugged in?!
8.    Static electricity could not explain Uzzah's death.
9.    If Uzzah died following an electric shock, the priests who carried the Ark would also have been electrocuted.
10.    The divine warning against unlawful touching extended to many sacred things, and not only the Ark. The Ark happened to be the one object that Uzzah touched.
11.    The cherubim figures were not microphone-type instruments. Exodus 25: 22 says that God would commune with Moses from BETWEEN the cherubim ABOVE the Mercy Seat.
12.    Von Daniken's idea of a magnet and a loudspeaker in association with the cherubim is technically impossible: even if von Daniken's idea of "electrically charged" was correct (it is not) only millionths part of one volt would be produced.
13.    This would be nothing like the great volume required for communication with a space ship.  Von Daniken's hypothesis is ludicrous.
14.    "Without actually consulting Exodus": such an approach indicates sloppy writing and unconvincing non-research.
15.    "I seem to remember" is not an acceptable approach if one has aspirations to be taken seriously by any but the gullible.

### An Incredible Extra Point

One incredible extra point must be given. In his book, *According to the Evidence* (pages 302-310), von Daniken has an elaborate description of what he calls "the manna machine" which was supposedly used to provide food for the Israelites in the wilderness. Von Daniken himself points out (as others have done) that the article on which his hypothesis is based first appeared in *The New Scientist on* 1 April, 1976. However, he disagrees with those who claim it was an April Fool's day joke, and says that the authors (George Sassoon and Rodney Dale) have since published the results of their research elsewhere. Von Daniken does not say if that "research" is the same as the *New Scientist* article.

However, the "incredible extra point" we refer to is at page 309 of von Daniken's book. He tells us that after the capture of Jericho "the machine was put in a silo as a holy object (1 Samuel 4:3). Later it was captured by the Philistines, but brought back very quickly, because it killed many of them. Naturally. The Philistines had never seen the manna machine working, nor had they obtained any instructions for use when they pinched the apparatus. It has always been thus. Technology with which people are unfamiliar is dangerous."

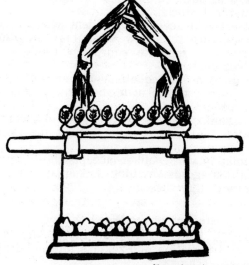

—Drawing by Lynette Hallihan
**The Ark of the Covenant.**
In *Chariots Of The Gods?* it was said to be electrically charged.
Now we find it is a storehouse for the "manna machine" the
Israelites used on their wilderness journey!!!

He then tells us, "David put it in a tent as a ritual object, and Solomon had a temple built for the mysterious machine (2 Chronicles 2: 5)."

So the Ark of the Covenant is now a dangerous manna machine! We saw above that it was electrically charged — that was yesterday's version. Today it is a dangerous machine. What nonsense will this man produce about the Ark of the Covenant tomorrow?

### Misusing the Text

We have shown elsewhere in this book that in his elaboration of the record about Ezekiel and the space ship, von Daniken leaves out "I saw visions of God." This was so in *Chariots Of The Gods?*, and also in the debate at North Dakota. That is hardly acceptable as a method of using source material.

### "No Reputable Historian would . . ."

In *Some Trust In Chariots* B. Thiering has an article called "The Chariots and the Dead Sea Scrolls," and her summary is well put. She says:
"No reputable historian would:
  (a)  treat evidence as independent when it was not;
  (b)  claim texts as new when they are not;
  (c)  combine separate sources without acknowledgment; or
  (d)  fail to deal adequately with accepted opinion contrary to his own about the nature of his sources.
"Von Daniken, by his grave methodological errors, discredits all that he has to say about the Dead Sea Scrolls."

Unfortunately von Daniken accepts those parts that suit him, and disregards anything that appears to oppose his preconceived hypotheses.

•

### A Distortion of the Word "Vision"

QUESTION: How do you approach Mr. von Daniken's translation of Ezekiel's interpretation of "the spaceship"?

QUESTION: Erich von Daniken, in your stand about Ezekiel in the Bible, do you know that it was a vision or how does this point by Mr. Wilson affect your views of the situation?

WILSON: We have commented on Mr. von Daniken's "interpretation of the spaceship" but there is one other point in the first of the two questions above, and that relates to the word "translation." In *According To The Evidence* at page 299 Mr. von Daniken quotes Ezekiel 43: 1-4. He ignores the setting of the series of incidents, given at Ezekiel 40: 1-2 where we read,

"In the twenty-fifth year of our exile, in the beginning of the year, on the tenth day of the month, in the fourteenth year after the city had been smitten, on that very day the hand of the Lord was upon me,

"And in visions of God He brought me into the land of Israel."

It is clearly stated that it is "IN VISIONS OF GOD." Ezekiel is in captivity in Babylon, but he now is shown BY VISION, an ideal situation associated with A FUTURE temple in Jerusalem. IT SHOULD BE UNDERSTOOD THAT AT THIS TIME THE TEMPLE IN JERUSALEM WAS IN UTTER RUINS. Nebuchadnezzar saw to that in 587 B.C. and Ezekiel gives us the date of his own vision, "the 25th year of our exile" (Ezekiel 40: 1, above). The first captives were taken into exile in 606 B.C., and so Ezekiel's experience is related to a time some years AFTER the Temple had been destroyed and it was STILL in ruins (before the return from exile).

In that series of visions Ezekiel describes a restored Temple, in a similar way to another prophetic vision given in Revelation, the last Book of the Bible. The passage quoted by von Daniken is clearly part of that series of visions—

— BUT —

**Von Daniken Translates the Word "Vision" as "Mobile Vessel" (!)**

at page 299 of *According To The Evidence.*

At Ezekiel 43: 3 Ezekiel says, "The VISION which I saw," and von Daniken translates that as "and the MOBILE VESSEL which I saw" (*According To The Evidence*, page 299).

I happen to have a Divinity degree, and am academically qualified in both Hebrew and Greek. The word used at Ezekiel 43: 3 is marah, which has behind it the idea of SEEING. Strong's *Exhaustive Concordance Of The Bible* describes it as being a form of marah, which relates to the act of seeing, and the actual descriptive words are:

"A VISION; also (causative) a MIRROR — looking glass, vision."

For von Daniken to translate marah as "mobile vessel" is, to say the least, clearly going beyond the meaning of the word. He further says (same page), "It says clearly in the text that the space ship went into the temple."

Rubbish!

As to the second question, Does Mr. von Daniken "know that it was a vision?" — in the debate von Daniken specifically stated that Ezekiel was NOT having visions.

One wonders why he omitted the words, "I saw visions of God," both in *Chariots Of The Gods?* and in his reading of Ezekiel at North Dakota.

Let us make it clear that Ezekiel says in that earlier incident of Ezekiel Chapter 1 that it WAS a vision. In that vision, God was not IN a space ship but is clearly depicted as being OUTSIDE and ABOVE the so-called "vehicle." The God of the Bible is not a Being Who needs to use a space ship to move around the world or the universe!

●

QUESTION: I agree it was a vision: was Ezekiel by chance explaining something in the future?

Ezekiel has a whole series of visions in his prophecy, and undoubtedly they look to the future. In Chapter 37 he describes a valley of dry bones that come to life, and this is usually taken as a picture of the revived nation of Israel. Undoubtedly much that Ezekiel wrote looked into the future.

### Did Ezekiel See a Spaceship?

Clearly, there is great interest in Ezekiel's vision. Here is a summary of some relevant points.

See Chapter 6 *Crash Go The Chariots* and Chapter 3 *The Space Gods Revealed.*

1.   According to von Daniken not only did Ezekiel see a space vehicle, but the gods "took him with them in their vehicle." (*Chariots Of The Gods?* p. 57.) However, Ezekiel said it was a vision. Both in *Chariots Of The Gods?* and in the debate at North Dakota Erich von Daniken omitted the words "I saw visions of God" as he quoted from Ezekiel Chapter 1. The chapter also makes it clear that God Himself is OUTSIDE the so-called

spacecraft — He is clearly so depicted.

2.   Ezekiel himself is referred to in Chapter 12 as being a sign to his people, a living symbol (Ezekiel 12: 11).

3.   At the debate von Daniken insisted that Ezekiel was not seeing a vision.  The fact is, however, that the Bible itself says this was a vision.  We have a representation of the powers of God in symbolic form, a form that goes some way towards helping us to understand the transcendence of God, and to understand some of the mysteries associated with God.  The greatness of Almighty God can hardly be explained in human terminology, and the difficulties are by no means eased by methods such as that of Erich von Daniken when he omits the words "I saw visions of God."

4.   He further omits the statement in Ezekiel describing the throne on which God sat above the so-called vehicle, and not in it.  By von Daniken's interpretation, God must be literally sitting in human form on a throne in the sky, visible to humans such as Ezekiel.

5.   Von Daniken sees the description in Ezekiel 1: 15-19 as applying to several helicopters, and quotes Josef Blumrich, formerly Chief of the Systems Layout Branch at the Marshall Space Flight Center of NASA.  He wrote a book called *The Space Ships Of Ezekiel,* and Ronald Story aptly says (at page 19) that it "can only be described as an extreme form of rationalization, with a good supply of technical jargon and diagrams."  Story points out that von Daniken was delighted to have such an outstanding technician take his speculations literally, but, as Story suggests, "that Blumrich has done so shows the fascination *Chariots Of The Gods?* holds for our technologically-oriented society" (p. 20).

6.   Von Daniken has the four faces depicted by Ezekiel as associated with four helicopter-type vehicles, based on what Josef Blumrich has suggested.  God is omnipresent, and if we limit Him to helicopter-type vehicles they certainly cannot go in all directions at once in an omnipresent sense.  They are physical machines, and therefore they must break, no matter how strong they are.  To suggest that Ezekiel was describing four helicopter-type vehicles is nonsense.

7.   In *According To The Evidence* (p. 299) von Daniken translates the word "vision" as "mobile vessel," quoting Ezekiel 43: 3.  What a strange liberty with the text!

QUESTION: Dr. Wilson, how do you know that
the Bible is the only accurate ancient writing,
of which the other writings (Gilgamesh) are but
fragments?   Maybe it's the other way around.

(See above re the *Epic of Gilgamesh*, and what follows
below.)

QUESTION: Why are traditional religionists so
sure the Biblical accounts are so accurate rela-
tive to myths of other cultures, and is this
scientific? (See below.)

QUESTION: Dr. Wilson, how can you be so sure
that the archaeological knowledge we have is
complete?   You can't deny the writing of ancient
cultures.

(See re the *Epic of Gilgamesh* above, and what follows
below.)

## Archaeology and the Bible

The answer to such questions could involve another
book — in fact, my book *That Incredible Book — The
Bible* deals with questions such as this.   In *Crash Go The
Chariots* we have a chapter dealing with archaeology and
the Bible, and there we make four points:
  (a) Archaeology has confirmed the accuracy of
      many Bible incidents and stories;
  (b) Archaeology shows that many customs of an-
      cient peoples are recorded in the Scriptures;
  c) Archaeology has added to our knowledge of
      peoples and lands of the Bible; and
  (d) Archaeology has endorsed the meaning of many
      words and phrases which previously were un-
      known.
In *That Incredible Book — The Bible* we deal with
the way archaeology has thrown light on personalities
and people such as Abraham and Moses, the Canaanites
and the Assyrians, Christ and the Jews.
We discuss controversial incidents such as the great
flood and the destruction of Sodom and Gomorrah.   We
are able to show how scholars now realize that the visit
of the Queen of Sheba to King Solomon was not something in the nature of the *Tales of the Arabian Nights*.
We look at the Bible as history, showing how archaeology

has touched culture, customs, and languages in the Bible. We elaborate the findings from great libraries of other peoples, and from the cultures of various peoples who were Israel's neighbors.

Bible writers know about the gods of neighboring peoples, and about their various customs. They are able to give all sorts of connecting links between kings and rulers in various countries such as Babylonia, Egypt, Syria, Assyria, Israel and Judah, confidently telling of details that could not have been known except to eye-witnesses. The evidence for the genuineness of the Bible writings is remarkable, and is in a very different category from other so-called religious texts.

## Sensational Tablets from Ebla

The recent findings at Ebla are elaborated in Wil son's book *Ebla Tablets — Secrets Of A Forgotten City,* and they are again a great evidence of the way in which the Bible records stand investigation. From Ebla we have several copies of a creation tablet that is close to important concepts put forward in Genesis, such as:

   (i)  One "great one" (Lugal) who creates — not many "gods" as in other non-Biblical records;

  (ii)  He speaks and it is done ("fiat" creation); and

 (iii)  He creates from nothing.

The Genesis record is still vastly superior.

At Ebla we even have a reference to Sodom and Gomorrah and the other "Cities of the Plain," in the same order as they are mentioned in the Biblical record.

## New Light on New Testament Records

Other Wilson books deal with different aspects of the impact of archaeology, such as *New Light On The Gospels* and *New Light On New Testament Letters.* These are dealing with the papyrus finds, finds which made it forever clear that the New Testament documents were genuinely set against the backgrounds claimed for them. New Testament records are not myths and legends, but are actual records of history, set against the back-grounds claimed for them by the Bible writers themselves.

One important conclusion is that the prophecies that the Old Testament writers gave were also genuine. They did look on to the birthplace of Jesus the Christ, they did tell of how He came to be a light in Galilee, and that He would die by crucifixion and then rise again.

**Chapter 16:**

# FIFTY OTHER POINTS — AND THAT "CROUCHING ASTRONAUT"

Many other points could be made to show the unacceptability of Erich von Daniken's writings. My friend John Weldon (co-author in two other books) has drawn up a list. With his permission, the following are taken from that list, in the main avoiding topics already discussed in this present writing. Each point could be elaborated, but we have exhausted our space!

1. The Incas were not in Peru until 1200 A.D., not 3000 B.C. as von Daniken claims. Dr. Ann Kendall has worked in the area for ten years, and is an expert on Inca building techniques. In "The Case of the Ancient Astronauts" she shows that the Incas were expert stone workers and superb administrators. She commented that it was absolutely nonsense to think of the Incas and primitive people in the same way. In Sacsahuaman alone they organized 20,000 people per annum for their mighty construction works. (Von Daniken refers to the 200-ton stone there as being 20,000 tons! — in *Chariots Of The Gods* p. 22.)

2. "Even a cursory reading of the Gilgamesh Epic would dispel such absurd notions" as nuclear radiation being the poisonous breath that slew Enkidu.

3. The Sumerian King List was not perpetuated on seals and coins, but on clay tablets.

4. The fall of man and original sin are interpreted as man's lapse into having sex with animals.

5. The angels who saved Lot were robots, according to von Daniken.

6. Genesis 28: 12 telling us about "Jacob's ladder" may be an account of loading material into a space ship; this is another von Danikenism.

John Weldon has taken the following points from the evidence given in *Some Trust In Chariots*, B. Thiering and E. Castle, eds. The text used is the Corgi paperback edition, 1971, London. The book is a collection of 16 essays by specialists in various fields. The pages are first von Daniken's *Chariots Of The Gods?* then Castle's book.

7. The "Helwan cloth" does NOT require a modern special factory with great technical know-how in order to make it (page 27 Bantam ed.). The process was known 2,000 years ago (page 8).

8. The structure of the blocks of the Great Pyramid is limestone (soft), not granite (hard). (Von Daniken page 85, Castle page 10.)

9. The "non-existent" rope (page 101) can be seen in Cairo and several other museums. The non-existent rollers, grain and huts are also well attested. (Castle pages 10-11, 35.)

10. The ancient Egyptians DID import wood (page 97), from at least 9 different countries. (Castle page 11.)

11. The original height of the Pyramid of Cheops was 481.4 feet, not 490 (page 102; Castle page 11).

12. The area of the base of the Pyramid of Cheops divided by twice its height DOES NOT give pi (pages 99; 12).

13. The stone blocks were NOT joined to a thousandth of an inch (pages 100; 12).

14. Granite was cut and used, sparingly, in early Egyptian Dynasties (pages 5; 11).

15. The blocks of the Cheops Pyramid averaged $2\frac{1}{2}$ tons, NOT 12 tons (page 84, Castle).

16. Modern engineers COULD build a copy of Cheops; it could easily have been built in the lifetime of a Pharaoh, not 664 years; von Daniken's mathematical calculations are erroneous (pages 100, 101, 179; Castle page 85). (The Japanese have recently proved it can be done, with their widely publicized modern construction of a small pyramid in Egypt.)

17. Von Daniken's numbers relating to the Mayan calendar accuracy are at odds with each other (pages 125, 75; and Castle page 16).

18. The Greenbank Formula is NOT "far removed from mere speculation" (page 141 Bantam). There is considerable uncertainty regarding six of the seven factors in the formula, relating to the doubts about the existence of planets. The values chosen for "L" at the conference were based on much guess-work and were LESS THAN 20, not MORE than 40, as von Daniken claims (page 166). "No one really knows the value of most of the factors" (Castle page 17).

19. Velikovsky claimed that Venus came from JUPITER, not Mars (page 155; Castle page 18).

20. Von Daniken says electricity was unknown to the ancient Egyptians, but that the remains of an electric battery were found in Mesopotamia. (Castle page 37.)

21. Elephantinos in Greek does not mean "elephant," it means "ivory." The island that he says looks like an elephant from the air, does not. (Page 85; Castle pp. 37, 38.)

22. The Egyptian mummification technique was not imparted by astronauts who knew how to raise the dead (Castle page 38).

23. The Olmec sculpture heads are displayed in museums and CAN be transported — one was recently transported thousands of miles to New York for a special exhibition. (Page 117; Castle page 51.)

24. The most ancient text on Teotihuacan is not "ancient," but is from the end of the 16th century A.D. It does NOT mention that the gods assembled there to discuss mankind before *homo sapiens* existed. (Page 120; Castle page 52.)

25. The tall statues on top of the Pyramid of Tlahuizcalpantecuhtli are wearing feathered head dresses, NOT space helmets; protective breastplates worn in war, NOT advanced units; and the "communication devices" are atlatls or spear throwers. (Film; Castle page 53.)

26. The two wells at Chichen Itza are not identical, nor perfectly round. The wells are formed naturally when a limestone land-surface collapses over underground water. They were not caused by meteorites or rockets blasting off. (Pages 126-7; Castle page 54.)

27. The line drawing in *Return To The Stars* (now *Gods From Outer Space*) depicts Toltec, not Mayan, priests performing sacrifice to the sun god who required human hearts to sustain it and keep it on its course through the heavens. It does not refer to a misunderstood surgical technique of the space visitors. (Page 87 *Gods From Outer Space*; Castle pages 54-5.)

28. The Aztec drum huehuetl is not a space vehicle (film) and their other type of drum, teponaztli, does not depict a circular space ship. (Film and *Return To The Stars*; Castle page 55.)

29. The Toltec god Quetzalcoatl is EARLIER in origin than the Mayan god Kukulcan, and the accounts of Quetzalcoatl are Toltec, not Mayan. The Mayans des-

cribe only Kukulcan. (Pages 127-8; Castle page 56).

30. The representations of winged gods in Egypt are obviously bird wings, not rocket wings. (Castle page 72.)

31. Von Daniken's statements referring to the third, fifth, seventh, and eighth tablets of the Gilgamesh Epic are NOT in the Epic itself. (Pages 65 ff; Castle page 76.)

32. The evidence von Daniken gives to support the Sumerian Flood story over the Biblical one disproves his own argument. (Page 40; Castle page 77.)

33. All the cuneiform texts from Ur do NOT tell about gods. "I know of no cuneiform text from any city which would match the author's description of what occurs in every Ur text." "No part of this description of the Ur texts finds any basis in fact." (Page 40; Castle pages 78-9.)

34. Sumerian gods WERE represented in anthropomorphic form. (Page 42; Castle pages 79 and 11.)

35. "From the point of view of the Mesopotamian evidence this book is so full of error, mis-statement, untruth, as to be worthless" (Dr. Noel Weeks in Castle, page 80).

## Errors Relating to Light Years

36. His computation of the number of miles in a light year is off by a factor of 60. (Page 15; Castle page 119.) Also, in *Gods From Outer Space* (Bantam, page 4), IT WOULD TAKE 160,000 YEARS, NOT 80, TO REACH THE NEAREST STAR.

37. He gives no direct instance of an "artefact from space" (Castle, page 119).

38. Scientists do not know that tachyons MUST exist (Bantam, page 116). They may exist (Castle, page 121).

39. Mars did not once possess an advanced civilization, nor is Phobos an artificial satellite. (Page 154; Castle page 15.)

40. Jonathan Swift does NOT give "precise" data about Mars' two Moons — he is off by a large factor. (Pages 152-3; Castle page 18.)

41. In quoting Einstein's theory of relativity in one place to support his theory (pages 22-3, 165), he undermines his argument in other places (page 164; Castle page 18).

42. If the "gods" are so advanced, as Von Daniken claims, why are the pictures he uses similar to OUR technology? (Page 97; Castle pages 20-21.)

43. Von Daniken admits: "The Pentateuch . . . is a mine of information for my theory, so long as the texts are read imaginatively, with the eyes of a man living in the age of space travel." (Unfortunately, too many other authors are attempting to do the same.) However, how can he trust something he himself believes is unreliable? "The Old Testament is a wonderful collection of laws and practical instructions for civilization, of myths and bits of genuine history" (Gods From Outer Space, Bantam 1974, page 155). In Chariots Of The Gods? he remarks: "The Bible is full of . . . contradictions" (Bantam 1973, page 40). So how do "myths" and "contradictions" support his theory?

44. "The millions of people all over the world (including China) who are obviously eager to accept his (von Daniken's) theories make up one of the most amazing phenomena of a world that seems to be looking for new gods to worship." "The great geographical religions — Hinduism, Christianity, Islam — may well be 'passe'," says von Daniken. "I expect that a new religion will arise, a religion of the unknown, indescribable, indefinable, something we cannot understand." (Newsweek, October 8, 1973, page 104.)

45. "A potentially viable scientific hypothesis should be capable of standing upon its own feet, relying upon the observed data and carefully formulated, logically derived inferences which themselves are capable of independent analysis." (Phillip Grause, Some Trust In Chariots, page 118.)

46. In von Daniken's third book, Gold Of The Gods, he claims to have seen a vast zoo or underground depository of gold animal statues and gold leaf documents in caves beneath Peru and Ecuador. Newsweek (above) comments: "Juan Moricz, a Hungarian-born Argentine adventurer who claims to have discovered the Ecuadorian caves, says von Daniken was never actually inside them."

47. Dr. Edwin M. Yamauchi (Specialist in Ancient History, Professor of History at Miami University, Oxford, Ohio) writes in Eternity magazine of January, 1974:

"No matter how appealing they may be to the uninformed reader, his suggestions are incredibly wild speculations without any factual basis . . . His remarks about Egypt and the Egyptians betray ignorance about even the most elementary facts.

"Von Daniken's misuse of evidence from Mesopotamia borders on madness."
48. Yamauchi remarks that von Daniken does not appear
to have even an elementary orientation to ancient history.
49. Carl Sagan (Professor of Astronomy and Dir. of the
Laboratory for Planetary Studies at Cornell University):
    "The book (*Chariots Of The Gods?* — Ed.) is
    absolutely dreadful. The only thing worse is the
    ABC documentary on the subject (Ancient Astro-
    nauts). ABC's program had every conceivable
    error." (In *Science News*, Nov. 3, 1973, p. 35.)
50. Dr. Herbert Alexander, Professor of Archaeology at
Simon Fraser University in Burnaby, British Columbia,
commented that "almost nothing in von Daniken's book,
related to archaeology, is factually correct." (In pamphlet
from Bible Science Association, Vancouver.)
    Much more could be added. The evidence is surely
overwhelming. Erich von Daniken's books should NOT
be taken seriously.

●

### That "Astronaut" about to Blast Off

A question was asked about the Palenque "astronaut." As this is one of von Daniken's most forceful
arguments, the following critique is highly relevant.

In *Chariots Of The Gods?* (pp. 100-101) Erich von
Daniken has this to say: "There sits a human being,
with the upper part of his body bent forward like a racing
motor-cyclist; today any child would identify his vehicle
as a rocket . . . The crouching being himself is manipu-
lating a number of undefinable controls and has the heel
of his left foot on a kind of pedal. His clothing is appropriate: short trousers with a broad belt. . . . And
there it is with the usual indentations and tubes, and
something like antennae on top. Our space traveller —
he is clearly depicted as one — is not only bent forward
tensely, he is also looking intently at an apparatus hanging in front of his face."

In that same context von Daniken argues that if
this example is not accepted as proof by scholars, then
we must doubt their integrity. He even tells us, "A gener-
ally unprejudiced look at this picture would make even
the most die-hard skeptic stop and think." What nonsense!

## What are the Facts?

1.    The original relief comes from a tomb at the Mayan ceremonial center of Palenque in Mexico.   It is carved on the lid of a sarcophagus.

2.    It was found in 1953, and not 1935 as von Daniken originally claimed.

3.    The astronaut has bare feet, and possibly no jacket at all.   We can count his toes — the first bare-footed astronaut?   And why no protective gloves on his hands?

4.    He is wearing the usual Mayan shorts, and this means that parts of his legs are also not covered.

5.    We wonder why he has other typical Mayan-type clothing, including anklets, bracelets and necklace.

6.    His head is outside the so-called rocket.

7.    His antenna is no more than the usual Mayan hairdo.

8.    The national bird of Guatemala, the quetzal bird, is perched on the top of the "rocket."

9.    Serpents are depicted . . . space travellers also?

10.    The rocket is actually a throne-chair, with its various components, such as side arm-rest and supporting back, easily recognized.

11.    Such thrones were used by Mayans and other dignitaries of neighboring peoples for transport across the country by relays of slaves.

12.    These dignitaries had to travel many miles, and for the sake of comfort would sit at various angles.   Such reclining is shown on this picture.

13.    The inscription is dated to approximately A.D. 683, based on interpretation of accompanying Mayan glyphs. At other sites von Daniken's single visits by astronauts are supposed to have taken place at much earlier times.

14.    In a debate with this author in Melbourne he had stated that there was only one visit, though later he has suggested that there were more. (His so-called "third visit" in historical times was "in Biblical times" which appears to extend to 683 A.D.!)

15.    We actually know the name of the ruler — Pacal.

16.    In von Daniken's picture the "astronaut" has his head protruding outside the so-called rocket — it is just as well the rocket is in fact only a throne chair after all! Otherwise it would be blasted off, if Mr. von Daniken's hypothesis were correct.

17.    Beneath the seat of the "astronaut" is the "earth monster" who is supposedly the guardian of the under-

world. This is a typical relief, and has nothing to do with astronauts. It is a ruler honored at his death.

18. The ruler's skeleton was actually found inside the sarcophagus. (Perhaps the rocket didn't fire after all!)

19. In this scene he is depicted as being in a state of suspension between two worlds, those of the living, and the dead. His so-called helmet is a representation of a corn plant. It is all fitting as religious symbolism on the lid of the dead man's sarcophagus. Now he is taking a dignified journey, with the traditional symbols of heaven and earth around him.

20. The Temple of the Inscriptions at Palenque was in fact a royal tomb. The scene carved on the stone slab actually has considerable religious significance. Nature worship was a basic part of Mayan religion, with corn plants and various fruits important in the understanding of the resurrection of the dead. This pointed on to the promise of immortality for man.

21. Jade was found on the ankles, wrists, and neck of the man inside the sarcophagus — and this contradicts von Daniken's claim in *Chariots Of The Gods?* that jade comes only from China. Jade has been found at other sites, such as some in Mexico and North America.

22. Von Daniken says that "today any child would identify his vehicle as a rocket," and refers to the "darting flame" at the tail. This actually is a two-headed serpent draped over the corn plant symbol and some large corn leaves. The "darting flame" probably represents the roots of the corn plant.

23. "It is not our fault that the stone relief from Palenque exists," says von Daniken on the very last page of *Chariots Of The Gods?* That is true, and its very existence gives the opportunity for an honest re-appraisal by von Daniken IF he really believes this is an astronaut figure, which it clearly is not.

24. A comparison of the same figure in *Chariots Of The Gods?* and then in *According To The Evidence* shows that von Daniken has turned the picture 90° in the second book, and now the "astronaut's" seat is at a right-angle to the floor!

25. Von Daniken has also cropped the picture, so that the arms and back-rest can no longer be seen. One wonders if he has a closed mind against explanations that oppose his pet theories.

# Chapter 17:

# A CONCLUDING SURVEY

A systematic analysis of all of Erich von Daniken's mistakes would take another book, and that is not necessary.

### A Survey of Other Errors

Frankly, I have been forced to some regrettable conclusions about his writings. I have been surprised and disturbed at the man's non-scholarly approach to what surely should be a scholarly exercise. One clear example is the figure of the so-called astronaut at Palenque. Comparison of the two pictures (first in *Chariots Of The Gods?* and then in *According To The Evidence*) shows that the second is cropped. It has been strongly pointed out to him that this is NOT a space-vehicle, and that the design of the chair can be clearly traced. Now the picture is cropped in the later book — there is no chair visible for the discerning researcher to see.

Von Daniken protests at the way he has been attacked, but this example illustrates why.

### Von Daniken's Literary Style

What then do we say as we end this survey? Some conclusions are listed below.

Erich von Daniken's own conclusions cannot be taken seriously, nor can his hypotheses be substantiated.

Scientists and other scholars are attacked, their integrity denied, their learning put casually to one side. Instead of such wrongly-based traditional views, the reader is encouraged to accept von Daniken himself as the great authority. He openly acknowledges that he has no formal tertiary education, and identifies himself with the reader as one of those who knows only too well that the scholars have some sort of a conspiracy. They have secret conferences, they distort facts, and refuse to change their point of view when the evidence so demands — even to the point of daring to call von Daniken's own theory "nonsense."

There is little systematic treatment of a subject: indeed, his writings teem with hundreds of subjects. Erich von Daniken is able to speak for archaeologists and historians, astronomers and engineers, cartographers and mathematicians, physicists and physicians — and of course theologians. A chapter in *Chariots Of The Gods?* highlights the question, "Was God An Astronaut?"

Mysteries are collected, and now they are no longer mysteries — for von Daniken has one simple answer to all those problems of Easter Island and the Pyramids, the Mayas and the Incas. Astronauts have visited the earth, taught the primitive earth-dwellers certain essential skills, then moved back to where they came from — whether it was Mars, the Pleiades, or some other unknown destination. Von Daniken suggests each of these three, so we do have some measure of choice! On his first Australian visit he stated that there was ONE visit from the astronauts, and that they were still on their way back to their home "out there." On his latest lecture tour in Australia there were THREE such visits in pre-historical and ancient times. He changes like the proverbial wind!

## How Not to Write!

Erich von Daniken introduces extraneous arguments from which he makes suppositions that are subtly close to the point discussed, but in fact he is guilty of *non sequiturs* (logical fallacies): he draws conclusions that are totally unwarranted by his argumentation.

He confuses time periods, bringing thousands of years together as though they dealt with simultaneous events.

He has a large number of uncorroborated statements.

He correlates cultures that are in fact separated by great distances of both time and space.

He does not recognize the native intelligence of humans in all ages and in all cultures.

He refuses to utilize Occam's Razor, the principle that the simplest explanation is usually the one to accept.

He acknowledges that he puts out some things "to be provocative," an unacceptable approach if he is to be taken seriously.

He contradicts his own statements from time to time.

He builds way-out conjectures on "mysteries" that are very often mysteries of his own making.

He takes unconnected facts and channels them into his own pre-conceived hypotheses, weaving a semblance of connection around facts and incidents that are not related.

He accepts only facts that suit those hypotheses.

He distorts evidence to make it fit those hypotheses.

He brushes aside opposing evidence.

He belittles scholarship when that scholarship is opposed to his own hypotheses.

He flatters his readers — "THEY know better!" — and presumes they are with him against supposedly inflexible scholars.

He confuses chronological and geographic data.

He ignores the great technological achievements of men who lived thousands of years ago — those achievements can be accounted for only by astronaut intervention, he says.

He appears to know little of great engineering and other activities of our forefathers.

Erich von Daniken has sensed the human urge for an explanation "from beyond," and has shown very real "psychological" discernment and commercial acumen. He reaches masses of people by his superficially exciting explanations, especially by his insistence on other-world visitors.

Man is so created that he has a desire to find what is beyond himself, a god or gods whose power is greater than that of man himself. For the one who rejects the God of the Bible, Erich von Daniken offers a plausible, but totally unconvincing, alternative. Something similar can be seen in the Old Testament as the Israelites turned to Baal when they did not want to accept the holy standards of Yahweh. Baal was a false god of the heavens, the god of lightning and thunder. The parallels are closer than might at first be obvious.

His writings are blasphemous and dangerous because of their seeming challenge to spiritual realities. They are unfortunate as an affront to scholarship because of their subtle overtones that suggest new learning, but they use methodology, techniques, and even facts in ways that actually distort scholarship.

THE WAR OF THE CHARIOTS

## Why is Von Daniken Accepted?

Erich von Daniken is accepted by thousands because:

(a) He offers a new theology;

(b) he opposes scholars and scholarship, in such a way as to identify readers with himself — "we know better," is his flattering style;

(c) he offers delusion instead of reality to a world unwilling to accept spiritual verities, but forced to reject a materialistic concept of evolution;

(d) he offers a new "answer" to life's beginnings;

(e) he offers a new challenge of space-life to a newly space-conscious generation;

(f) his writings have co-incided with an increased "respectability" of the U.F.O. phenomenon;

(g) he replaces the frustrations of science by a pseudo-science, complete with von Danikenisms and mumbo-jumbo jargon;

(h) science has failed as a religion, and for many people von Daniken's plausible (but highly erroneous) hypotheses have filled the vacuum with nonsensical conjectures;

(i) not only does he offer a new creation, a new "god," and a new "science," he also offers a new religion, with empty hypotheses that should be rejected by all men of truth.

## The Truth in a Nutshell

Carl Sagan was right when he wrote in the foreword to *The Space Gods Revealed:* "The popularity of von Daniken must, I think, be theological in origin."

The fact is, von Daniken's real attack is not only against archaeology, science, and scholarship. Ultimately that real attack, subtle as it is, is against—

The Bible

The God of the Bible

The creation recorded in the Bible

The Christ of the Bible; and

The hope offered by the Bible.

His case has failed, and his hypotheses have in no way detracted from the truths of the Bible nor from the teachings of Him Who said,

"I am the Way, the Truth, and the Life: no man comes to the Father, except through Me."

(John 14: 6)

## SOURCE MATERIAL AND BRIEF BIBLIOGRAPHY

1. Von Daniken's own books.
2. Wilson's own writings, including
   *Crash Go The Chariots;*
   *Gods In Chariots And Other Fantasies;*
   *The Chariots Still Crash;*
   *In The Beginning God;*
   *That Incredible Book, The Bible;*
   *New Light On The Gospels;*
   *New Light On New Testament Letters;*
   *U.F.O's And Their Mission Impossible.*
   Most are available from Word of Truth Productions, Box 288, Ballston Spa, N.Y. 12020.
3. Journal articles dealing with von Daniken material, as listed in this book at appropriate points. They include:
   *Encounter* Magazine; Ed. Melvin J. Lasky and Anthony Thwaite, London, Vol. XLI No. 2, August 1973. Article — *Anatomy of a World Best Seller — Erich von Daniken's Message from the Unknown.*
   Ferris, Timothy, *Playboy* interview with Erich von Daniken, August, 1974, pp. 51 ff.
   Mechanix Illustrated, September, 1977 (article, *The Crack In The Pyramid,* Bill D. Miller).
   Omohundro, John T., *Von Daniken's Chariots: A Primer in the Art of Cooked Science,* in *The Zetetic,* Journal of the Committee for Scientific Investigation of Claims of the Paranormal, Vol. 1 Nos. Fall/Winter 1976.
   Story, Ronald D., *Von Daniken's Golden Gods,* in *The Zetetic* (op. cit.), Vol. II No. 1, Fall/Winter 1977.
4. Refutations of von Daniken material by reputable authors in authoritative books; also books with relevant material, written independently of von Daniken. These include:
   *Aku-Aku,* Thor Heyerdahl, Pocket Books, N.Y., 1972 edition.
   *The Space Gods Revealed,* Ronald Story, Harper & Row, N.Y., 1976.
   *Chariots Of The Gods? — A Critical Review,* G. G. Garner, Australian Institute of Archaeology, Melbourne, Australia, 1972.
   *The Past Is Human,* Peter White, Angus & Robertson, Sydney, Australia, 1974.

*Some Trust In Chariots,* Ed. E. W. Castle and B. B. Thiering, Westbrooks Pty. Ltd., Perth and Sydney, Australia, 1972.

*The Pyramids Of Egypt,* I. E. S. Edwards, Pelican, Harmondsworth, 1961.

*Maps Of The Ancient Sea Kings,* C. H. Hapgood, Chilton Books, N.Y., 1966.

*Maya Civilization,* J. E. S. Thompson, University of Oklahoma, 1966.

*The Sirius Mystery,* Robert K. G. Temple, St. Martin's Press, New York, 1976.

Review of *The Sirius Mystery* by Michael W. Ovenden, Professor of Astronomy in the University of British Columbia, Vancouver, Canada: entitled *Mustard Seed of Mystery,* in *Nature,* Vol. 261, June 17, 1976.

*Red, White and Mysterious,* Stephen P. Maran, Researcher at N.A.S.A.'s Goddard Space Center in Greenbelt, Maryland, in *Natural History,* Aug.-Sept. 1975, Vol. 84, No. 7, pages 82, 86, 87.

*Noah's Three Sons,* Arthur C. Custance, Zondervan Publishing House, Grand Rapids, Michigan, 1975.

*The Australian Aboriginal Heritage,* Ed. R. M. Berndt and E. S. Phillips: Ure Smith in Assoc. with the Australian Society for Education Through the Arts, Sydney, Australia, 1973.

*Genetics And The Races of Man,* Wm. C. Boyd, Blackwell's Scientific Publications, 1950.

5. A quarter of a century of direct and indirect involvement with Biblical archaeology and tertiary education. The extensive references in *That Incredible Book, The Bible,* illustrate the width of years of reading which is typical of academic lecturers. In addition, personal correspondence with authorities in specific areas of investigation; information gained from other authorities at public lectures; and consultations with academic colleagues.

   Personal visits to many of the sites have also been important.

6. As we went to press, the television film "The Case of the Ancient Astronauts" was presented over Australian television. It is written and produced by Graham Massey and is an excellent critique of von Daniken's hypotheses.

# INDEX

Other books by Dr. Clifford Wilson are available from Master Books, Box 15666, San Diego, California 92115.

They include . . .

Crash Go The Chariots ... ... ... ... ... ... ... $1.95

The Occult Explosion ... ... ... ... ... ... ... ... $1.95

Crash Goes The Exorcist ... ... ... ... ... ... ... $1.95

The Passover Plot — Exposed ... ... ... ... ... $2.25

Jesus the Teacher ... ... ... ... ... ... ... ... ... $1.95

Ebla Tablets: Secrets of a Forgotten City ... ... ... $1.95

Monkeys Will Never Talk — or Will They? ... ... $3.95

Close Encounters — a Better Explanation ... ... $2.95
    (with John Weldon)

Approaching the Decade of Shock ... ... ... ... $5.95
    (with John Weldon)